T0355641

HEIDEGGER & THE MYTH OF
A JEWISH WORLD CONSPIRACY

HEIDEGGER

& THE MYTH

OF A

JEWISH WORLD

CONSPIRACY

PETER TRAWNY

TRANSLATED BY ANDREW J. MITCHELL

THE UNIVERSITY OF CHICAGO PRESS
CHICAGO & LONDON

PETER TRAWNY is professor of philosophy and founder and director of
the Martin Heidegger Institute at the University of Wuppertal in Germany.
He is the author of many books and editor of Martin Heidegger's *Black Notebooks*.
ANDREW J. MITCHELL is associate professor of philosophy at Emory
University and the author of *The Fourfold: Reading the Late Heidegger*.

Originally published as *Heidegger und der Mythos der
jüdischen Weltverschwörung*
© Vittorio Klostermann GmbH, Frankfurt am Main, 2014.
3rd, revised and extended edition 2014.

The University of Chicago Press, Chicago 60637
The University of Chicago Press, Ltd., London
© 2015 by The University of Chicago
All rights reserved. Published 2015.
Printed in the United States of America

24 23 22 21 20 19 18 17 16 15   1 2 3 4 5

ISBN-13: 978-0-226-30373-4 (cloth)
ISBN-13: 978-0-226-30387-1 (e-book)
DOI: 10.7208/chicago/9780226303871.001.0001

The translation of this work was supported by a grant from the Goethe-Institut,
which is funded by the German Ministry of Foreign Affairs.

Library of Congress Cataloging-in-Publication Data
Trawny, Peter, 1964– author.
[Heidegger und der Mythos der jüdischen Weltverschwörung. English]
Heidegger and the myth of a Jewish world conspiracy / Peter Trawny ;
translated by Andrew J. Mitchell.
pages cm
"Originally published as Hiedegger und der Mythos der jüdischen Weltverschwörung
© Vittorio Klostermann GmbH, Frankfurt am Main, 2014.
3rd, revised and extended edition 2014."
Includes bibliographical references and index.
ISBN 978-0-226-30373-4 (cloth : alk. paper) — ISBN 978-0-226-30387-1 (ebook)
1. Heidegger, Martin, 1889–1976—Views on Jews. 2. Antisemitism. 3. Jews—Identity.
I. Mitchell, Andrew J., 1970—translator. II. Title.
B3279.H49T639513 2015
193—dc23   2015014460

♾ This paper meets the requirements of ANSI/NISO
z39.48-1992 (Permanence of Paper).

To be German: to cast forth the innermost burden of
western history and to take it upon one's shoulder.

MARTIN HEIDEGGER, *Überlegungen* VII

/ / / / / / / / / / / / / /

And can you bear, Mother, as once on a time,
the gentle, the German, the pain-laden rhyme?

PAUL CELAN, "Nearness to Graves"

CONTENTS

////////////////////////////

As the discussions of Heidegger's anti-Semitism began earlier
this year with the publication of the philosopher's *Überlegungen*,
the first sequence of the *Black Notebooks*, the effect was unforesee-
able. That holds still today. The question is: what future is there
for a thinking that sees in "world Judaism" a destructive power
of history—a form of destruction that ultimately destroys history itself?

In the meantime, the first attempts (along with mine) to deal
with and delve into this question have appeared.[1] Other attempts
will certainly follow because the ongoing publication of the *Black
Notebooks* will confront us with further problematic statements
on Judaism and the Shoah. On the other hand, trusted voices
have remained silent. Thus the apologist branch of "Heideggerians" finds itself in a crisis—because in the face of the Heideggerian idea of "world Judaism" the usual defensive and reflexive
justifications of Heidegger are infinitely more difficult to pull
off than are the customary attacks on a thinker whom one has
always already assumed to be an anti-Semite. Renowned Heidegger scholars find themselves in an intellectual bunker seeking to
save whatever there is to save. The moral Inquisitors are the only
ones to triumph. Both answer these questions in their own way.

To have to speak of "Heidegger's anti-Semitism" is painful not only to the old devotees of this philosopher. Indeed, it has long been known that Heidegger shared banal anti-Semitic stereotypes with the majority not only of Germans, but perhaps even of Europeans. That he transformed these stereotypes into the history of being was hitherto unknown. This transformation, carried out at the end of the 1930s, is *the* problem.

The conflict is already under way in the very concept of anti-Semitism. Can one characterize Heidegger's ideas, which he himself most likely did not consider anti-Semitic, as anti-Semitic? This is unavoidable. In order to interpret Heidegger's statements an actual understanding of anti-Semitism is presumed. Even if we are aware of the fact that the significance of anti-Semitic ideas before the Shoah is not congruent with that of such ideas after the Shoah, historical relativism is out of the question.

Thus we cannot ignore that Heidegger's statements stem from a context in which the anti-Semitic stereotypes that he applied were all well-known. Even Heidegger's thought, unstated but implicit in his ideas, that the Jew would be *the* representative of the modern was widespread. It was even self-critically discussed by Zionists.[2] It is nevertheless clear that Heidegger took no notice of these discussions, where, for obvious reasons, Zionist viewpoints increasingly dominated the issue of assimilation. Heidegger had many Jewish students, but scarcely an interest in Judaism.

Heidegger denied himself such an interest, above all in the 1930s and 1940s, as he intellectually battled with Christianity. The decision for the early Greek thinkers and poets, the decision even for Hölderlin, was at the same time also a decision against the rigorous monotheism of the Jews and Christians. Hölderlin's turn of phrase "god of the gods," i.e., god of a differentiated sequence of "gods," also had an effect on Heidegger's thinking.[3] The phrase is simply incompatible with Judaism and Christianity.

One could object that an *anti*-Semitism could never come about in Heidegger's thinking since the philosopher constantly pointed out that every "anti-" necessarily depends upon what it rejects and battles. In point of fact, he emphasizes this in the *Überlegungen* as well.[4] But it does not follow that he thereby forgoes attacks against Judaism, much less against Christianity. If Heidegger here falls short of one of his own ideas, this is no rarity in philosophy. The mastery of the text has its limits.

Without having known something of Heidegger's ideas in these *Notebooks*, Emmanuel Levinas appears to have demarcated the central conflict between Heidegger's thinking and Judaism.[5] Here the terror before a universal technology, there the terror before the mythos of holy places and their gods. There the idea of a universal face of man, here the differentiation of the peoples into Greeks, Romans, Germans, Russians, French, English, Japanese, etc. The urgency of a confrontation with these oppositions has only intensified with the publication of the *Überlegungen*.

There have been and will be further attempts to diminish the significance of the *Black Notebooks* in the context of Heidegger's work as a whole. Do not the titles *Überlegungen* (Considerations), *Anmerkungen* (Remarks), *Vier Hefte* (Four Notebooks) already indicate that Heidegger minimized their importance? It is a hopeless attempt. Heidegger had always favored simple titles (*Contributions to Philosophy*, *Mindfulness*, even *Being and Time*), but then gave to later *Black Notebooks* the names *Vigiliae* and *Notturno*. With the publication of the *Black Notebooks* there appears in the collected works of Heidegger—alongside the being-historical treatises and the lecture courses and independent lectures—a further, distinctly esoteric dimension that stands in connection with these other two divisions of the collected works. Only the complete publication of the *Black Notebooks* will show to what extent Heidegger's thinking unfolded itself in "paths" and not works.

It is well-known that during the war years Heidegger also as-

cribed a specific role to Americans in his being-historical narrative: "The Americans, however, take the condition of nul-
lity as the promise of their future, since they indeed decimate
everything under the guise of 'happiness' for all. In Americanism, nihilism reaches its pinnacle."[6] This is scarcely to be distinguished from the role that Heidegger attributes to "world Judaism," even if the allusion to the "pursuit of happiness" from the
Declaration of Independence is a direct reference to American
history. The American reader not only of my book, but also of
the *Überlegungen*, will most likely be a Heidegger scholar. Such
ascriptions do not surprise him/her. But in the *Black Notebooks*
they assume a more specific shape when situated within a being-
historical topography.

Heidegger's thinking is perhaps *the* catastrophic echo in philosophy of the catastrophe that shook the twentieth century. It
may be that philosophy does not have the task of being a catastrophic echo. Nevertheless, the thinking of the twentieth century would be poorer were this echo not to reach us. It is unlikely
that it will fade away. Our only future lies in this echo of the
twentieth century.

Peter Trawny,
July 12, 2014

INTRODUCTION

A Thesis in Need of Revision

Leo Strauss, Hannah Arendt, Karl Löwith, Hans Jonas, Emmanuel Levinas, Werner Brock, Elisabeth Blochmann, Wilhelm Szilasi, Mascha Kaléko, Paul Celan—Jews who in one way or another each encountered Martin Heidegger. For them he was teacher, object of admiration, lover, revered thinker, supporter. It has been well established that, as a philosopher and teacher in the 1920s, Heidegger attracted "young Jews" to him; indeed, there was understood to be a general proximity between his thinking and Judaism.[1] The encounter with Jewish students after 1945 was painful, as with Celan, and torn between admiration and repulsion.[2] But without doubt there was also rapprochement. Arendt's return to Germany at the beginning of the 1950s was also a return to Heidegger.

Certainly there were worries. Jacques Derrida, also of Jewish origin, in a short text entitled "Heidegger's Silence," spoke of a "wounding of thinking," of "a silence after the war with regard to Auschwitz."[3] Heidegger did not express himself publicly on the Shoah. The public for him was no moral authority, rather the opposite. Heidegger spoke often of the "dictatorship of the public realm."[4] Silence, keeping silent, was for him a philosophical comportment. Did he ever speak of Auschwitz in his personal, intimate encounters? There are no accounts that tell of this, although there is a poem for Hannah Arendt, a single testament, that speaks of a "burden." But how much store should we set in a poem?

The worries did not lead to Heidegger's being accused of anti-Semitism. Rüdiger Safranski, in his influential biography, decisively proclaimed that Heidegger had not been an anti-Semite.[5] Up to now, this has been the prevailing opinion, one that supplies the important apologist thesis: Heidegger was indeed involved with National Socialism, for a longer or shorter period of time as some would have it, but he was not an anti-Semite. Does his own biography not speak against this? How could someone be an anti-Semite who lived so freely with Jews and even had at least one "Jewish lover"?

Anti-Semitism was and is that which is directed against Jews, sprung from rumor, prejudice, and pseudoscientific sources (whether from race theory or simply racist), functioning affectively and/or administratively, and leading to (*a*) defamation, (*b*) universal vilification, (*c*) isolation: professional prohibitions, ghettoes, camps, (*d*) expulsion: emigration, (*e*) annihilation: pogroms, mass executions, death camps. Additionally, *today*, we also deem anti-Semitic anything that is supposed to characterize the Jew as "Jew." On the one hand, these various stages are not easily separated; on the other, I find it problematic to assume that a verbal defamation need end in the Shoah.[6]

A new look at Heidegger reveals a facet previously unknown: at a certain stage along his path, the philosopher admitted anti-Semitism into his thinking; more precisely, he admitted a *being-historical anti-Semitism* (seinsgeschichtlicher Antisemitismus).[7] There appears to be no doubt of this, as will be shown. But everything depends upon explaining what is meant by the concept "being-historical anti-Semitism." The primary intention of the following reflections is to develop a sense for this.

The introduction of such a concept must be well considered, for obviously it could have disastrous consequences. The "anti-Semite" is morally and politically finished—especially after the Shoah. The suspicion of anti-Semitism could strike Heideggerian philosophy with great vehemence. How could it be that one of the greatest philosophers of the twentieth century was an advocate not only of National Socialism but also of anti-Semitism? Such a question is not easy to answer. It stigmatizes Heidegger's thinking and places us squarely before an enigma.

In Heidegger's case the further question arises of whether and to what extent anti-Semitism contaminates his philosophy as a whole. Does an anti-Semitic ideology so possess Heidegger's thinking that we would have to speak of an "anti-Semitic" philosophy? Would we then have to keep our distance from this philosophy because an "anti-Semitic philosophy" does not and cannot exist? After decades, would we not have to acknowledge that Heidegger's thinking is actually not a matter of "philosophy," or even of "thinking," but instead just an uncanny error? These questions are all to be answered in the negative, though no easy path leads to that answer.

The concept of "contamination" is particularly important for what follows. Anti-Semitism, which infests certain passages of the *Black Notebooks*, con-taminates it, brings one thing into contact with another. Consequently, the thinking that was previously conceived to be a matter of neutral theoretical insight now appears in a different light. This occurs because contamination takes hold at the margins of thinking, dissolving them, blurring them. And with this the topography of Heideggerian thought starts to waver. The interpretation ventured here positions itself in relation to this instability. It seeks to arrive at an answer to the question of how far this contamination reaches and how it is to be delimited.

The predicate "anti-Semitic" is particularly dangerous, because for the most part it is used to announce an ideological complicity with the Shoah. Do all paths of anti-Semitism lead to Auschwitz? No. The etiology of genocide is always problematic because it is always multiple. Heidegger's utterances about the Jews cannot be tied to Auschwitz. Nevertheless, even if there is no evidence that Heidegger approved of the "administrative mass murder" (Arendt) of the Jews, even if there is no indication of this, Heidegger must have known what took place in the death camps. Thus we can never entirely exclude the possibility that he held such violence against the Jews to be necessary. A thinking beyond good and evil follows its own necessities. This lasting possibility is what poisons particular statements of Heidegger's.

These previously unknown statements are found in the so-called *Black Notebooks*—a characterization coined and applied by Heidegger himself for thirty-four black, oilcloth notebooks in which, between roughly 1930 and 1970, he gave his thinking a unique form.[8] For the most part, they have simple titles like *Considerations, Remarks, Four Notebooks, Hints,* and *Preliminaries.* The titles *Vigiliae* and *Notturno* are unusual, not only in the context of the *Black Notebooks,* but in the whole of Heidegger's work. All notebooks bear Roman numerals. The entire collection of notebooks has not been completely preserved. *Überlegungen* I, the first notebook of all, is missing. What happened to the missing notebook is unknown.

The series of Roman numerals does not unconditionally follow the order of composition. This is so partly because Heidegger wrote in multiple notebooks at once. Since corrections are found in only a few places and the entries themselves are by no means merely aphoristic, we cannot assume they were written directly into the notebooks. Preparatory drafts must have existed but have not been retained. The texts we are concerned with are thus neither private jottings, nor even mere notes. Instead, we are dealing with revised philosophical writings.

According to information from Hermann Heidegger, his father had decided that the *Black Notebooks* were to be published as the conclusion to the *Gesamtausgabe* [the "Collected Edition" of Heidegger's works]. That decision was subsequently altered for good reasons. The manuscript is simply too important for its publication to be postponed by the arbitrary duration of other editorial projects. Martin Heidegger's decision appears to confirm this special role for the manuscript. Are the *Black Notebooks* something like his philosophical legacy?

The status of this unique manuscript in relation to the treatises both published (such as *Being and Time*) and unpublished (such as the *Contributions to Philosophy*), as well as to the lecture courses, essays, and lectures, depends on how we answer this question. If it were a philosophical legacy, then, in relation to all the other writings, it could be read as a kind of distillation, or foundational text, or even as both of these. Speaking in favor of this is that Heidegger makes continual reference to the *Black Notebooks* in the unpublished treatises. Speaking against it is that the *Notebooks* rarely achieve the philosophical intensity characterizing the *Contributions to Philosophy*, for example.

But the unique style of the *Black Notebooks* is part of their flavor. If one assumes that the unpublished treatises are esoteric texts, then these notebooks are still more intimate traces of Heideggerian thinking. The author who usually remains hidden now appears in the form of a persona. But how is such a personalization of the text possible at all, when the manuscript presents itself never as a diary or thought-journal, but instead always as a presentation of thought itself at its most authentic? Is the persona of the *Black Notebooks* yet another mask, behind which the philosopher hides—and not only from the public? In the disconcerting words that arise at times, especially in the 1930s, is he not also hiding from himself?

Does Heidegger's philosophy come to its culmination far from the public and at the edge of silence and stillness? In a postwar note Heidegger says of a particular observation that "in keeping with its essence," it would "no longer be said in public for a reader," but instead would belong "to the destiny of beyng [*Seyns*] itself and its stillness."[9] To write beyond the reader for the "destiny of beyng itself"? As we shall see, Heidegger himself ultimately contravenes this extreme stylization.

Nevertheless, this does throw a light on the *Black Notebooks* to be considered in what follows. It is a question of those notebooks that were composed before 1948. In these, and especially between 1938 and 1941, Heidegger comes to speak more or less directly of "the Jews." They are transposed into a being-historical topography or autotopography (since every location bears a corresponding relation to the self), in which they are assigned a particular and specific significance, one that is of an anti-Semitic nature.

Heidegger's anti-Semitic statements—enlisted into a philosophical context—are found exclusively in manuscripts that the philosopher wanted to withhold from the public for as long as possible. He even hid his anti-Semitism from the National Socialists.[10] Why? Because he was of the opinion that his brand of anti-Semitism was distinct from theirs. This is provisionally correct. Nevertheless, caution is advisable. Heidegger concealed not only his anti-Semitism from the public, but his thinking itself, as he explains already around 1935: "Thinking in the other beginning is not for the public."[11] The concealment of anti-Semitism is connected to a thinking that sees in the public only a perfect crime against philosophy.

The following considerations pursue an interpretation beyond that of apology, something of which Heidegger's work remains in need. They follow the above-mentioned movement of a contamination. Consequently, one judgment or another might appear too one-sided or even go astray. Coming discussions may well contradict or correct my interpretations. No one would be happier than I.

THE BEING-HISTORICAL
LANDSCAPE

In the years after *Being and Time*, Heidegger found himself in a philosophical crisis. This made itself known in various ways. It was not merely that the second part of *Being and Time* (as announced in § 8) was held back. But even the third division of part 1 was provided only after the fact in the form of a lecture course from the summer of 1927. The lecture courses that followed offered only tentative experiments. The project of an "absolute science of being" was not realized.[1] Similarly, the undertaking of a "metontology" remained just an unfinished torso.[2] The concomitant elaboration of a metaphysics of freedom likewise remained rudimentary.

Then something came to the philosopher that well-nigh revolutionized his thinking: a *narrative*.[3] Philosophy appeared frozen in lifeless positions. *Being and Time* was an academic success, to be sure, but this did not somehow mean that academic philosophy as a whole was moved by it. Heidegger viewed the unceasing proliferation of academic research with growing intolerance. The era itself had fallen into an economic crisis. It could not continue like this. Political changes announced themselves; first tentatively, then with violence.

Already in *Being and Time* the philosopher had elucidated what he understood by "destiny" (*Geschick*).[4] "Destiny" would be the "historizing [*Geschehen*] of the community, of a people." In "our Being with one another in the same world and in our resoluteness for definite possibilities," the life paths of these individuals "have already been guided in advance." "Only in communication and in struggling," does the "power of destiny become free." This would be the "sole authority which a free existing" could have.[5] For Heidegger "authentic Dasein" was constantly exposed to such a destiny. Were this destiny to remain outstanding, it would entail the fallenness of Dasein. Later, after 1945, this is exactly what he discerns as "nihilism": the "unhistoricalness" of "Americanism," i.e., the destruction of every "destiny."[6]

Thus as everything was drawing to an end, Heidegger began to look for the "beginning." Already in winter 1931-32 he held a lecture course that concerned the "beginning of Western philosophy" and the understanding of truth inherent in it.[7] In the first half of the course, Heidegger interprets Plato's cave analogy publicly for the first time. In the midst of the interpretation, Heidegger emphasizes that while "poison and weapons for death are indeed at the ready today" (referring to the death of Socrates by hemlock), nevertheless "the philosopher" is lacking. "Today" there are, "when it comes down to it, only better or worse sophists," who can "at best prepare the way for the philosopher who will come."[8] End and beginning align themselves with the coming of a philosopher and a philosophy beyond the sophistry of academic everydayness.

But the real lecture course of the beginning is the following one, from the summer of 1932. Heidegger referred to it later, saying that "since the spring of 1932 the basic features of the plan" had been established, which "received its first formulation in the project *Of the Event*."[9] This lecture course, notably an interpretation of Anaximander and Parmenides, begins with an invocation of the narrative:

Our mission: the demolition [*Abbruch*] of philosophizing? That is, the end of metaphysics through an original questioning concerning the "meaning" (truth) of beyng.

We want to seek out the *beginning* of Western philosophy.[10]

What Heidegger found was the narrative of an end and a beginning, which he would repeatedly reflect upon over the next decade and a half.

The departure that so energized Heidegger's philosophy at this moment was the possibility of no longer pursuing philosophy as a hermeneutics of historically canonical texts or of a historically canonical world. Instead—in a more decisive integration of *Being and Time*—Heidegger would link his thinking to the entire course of a European history that was revolutionary to its core. The beginning, which Heidegger increasingly found in the pre-Socratic thinking of Anaximander, Heraclitus, and Parmenides, had come to an end. "Sophists" made tired attempts at convincing each other to adopt historically ossified positions, and Heidegger himself appeared to have become one of these. Moreover, the political situation was volatile. One got the impression that the beginning needed repeating. What Heidegger expressed philosophically was not something limited to his thinking alone, but instead something that took place suddenly and world historically; and that—so it seemed to him—could be no accident.

In the passage just cited from the beginning of the lecture course from summer 1932, one finds a reference to *Überlegungen* II, i.e., the first *Black Notebook* that we have. There the thought of a demolition of philosophy is entertained:

Must we today, in the end, *break off* [abbrechen] *from philosophizing*—because people and race are no longer up to the task and as a result the force of these becomes increasingly withered and denigrated to the point of nonforce?

Or is the demolition totally unneeded, since for a long time now there has been nothing happening anyway?[11]

The choice is the following: we must break off from philosophy either because it stands in the end-situation of a distinctly atrophying history, or because it itself is already so atrophied as to preclude any further degradation. Ultimately, the two go together: the academic philosophy of the era was as weak as the era itself.[12]

One consequence could be a "flight into faith or some kind of raving blindness," with Heidegger understanding the latter as "rationalization or technologization." This and "faith" were naturally to be avoided. The "demolition" must happen otherwise. For the demolition was something that needed "to be *accomplished* just as much as the beginning—such that this cessation would have to be a most proper occurrence and the ultimate effort." Just as the beginning must be actualized, so the "demolition." What would have to be "demolished and ended," however, was "only that history of 'post-Greek' philosophy, poor in beginning and gone astray." From this occurrence an "opening of the beginning," a "beginning again," could arise. The narrative of the "first" and "other beginning"—accentuated by a "demolition"— was thereby found.[13]

It is the narrative of the "history of beyng," which Heidegger once summarized so:

> First beginning: Departure, (Idea), Machination.
> Other beginning: Event of Appropriation [*Ereignis*].

The whole would be "*beyng.*"[14] The narrative connects two beginnings and an end, which is characterized as "machination" (*Machenschaft*).[15] This "machination" is the "metaphysics" that is coming to its end, which in the "event of appropriation" is overcome (*überwunden*) or, more precisely, converted (*verwunden*). This is a loose definition. The "event," which Heidegger construes in various ways, cannot be stated in a word, if it can be expressed at all.[16]

This structure of the history of being, this narrative, is ambivalent. One version of the story unfolds into the relationship between origin and decline, i.e., fallenness, whereby such fallenness does not destroy the possibility of a specific repetition of the origin, but covers it over and refuses it. In this sense and as the end-formation of metaphysics, "machination" blocks our entry to a place where the "truth of beyng" might be experienced not merely *as* refused, but instead as purely occurring. From here, it is only a short step to a way of thinking that we can characterize as a *being-historical Manichaeism*.[17]

This "machination," i.e., modern technology, becomes an enemy, so to speak, of the opening of that other place. "Machination" must disappear, must destroy itself, so that this other—whether blocked or open—can occur. Around the year 1941 Heidegger thought that "*all* imperialism"—i.e., the political dynamic of all warring parties—would be "driven toward the *highest consummation of technology*." He foresees the "final act" of these events, that "the earth itself will explode and contemporary humanity disappear." This, however, would be "no misfortune, but rather the first purification *of being* from its deepest deformation by the precedence of beings."[18]

The use of the word "purification" is ambiguous: (1) The "purification" is a κάθαρσις, the element of an onto-tragic thinking by Heidegger in which being itself is regarded as tragic. In the context of tragedy, κάθαρσις plays an important role in the *Poetics* of Aristotle (1449b27). Excessive cases of lamentation and trembling lead to the purification of just such excitations. Κάθαρσις as a holy action antedates this.[19] (2) The "purification" is a liberation from a contaminant, from a stain, that could be

identified with "beings" as matter, as material. This thought recalls Neoplatonism, which, roughly stated, sees evil in matter
as such. (3) The "purification" is an annihilation of the foreign
body that obstructs the possible purity of what is one's own. *This*
purification, as one of beings, Heidegger rejects. Indeed, it is ultimately to be asked whether he could entirely escape the ideology
of this third sense of purification.

Accordingly, purification appears to concern "decisions between beings and beyng"—as if the difference between "beyng"
and "beings" posed a choice.[20] By the end of the 1930s, this narrative and the atmosphere surrounding it grow more intense in
Heidegger's thinking. The intensity of the supposed "decision"—
which is tantamount to a liberation of "beyng"—leads to a dependency on beings that is all the stronger, the more radically
Heidegger invokes this liberation.[21] The world war has left its
mark on this thinking. In the later version of Heidegger's thinking of technology, the possibility of a transformed relation to
"positionality" (*das Ge-Stell*) is found within positionality itself.[22]
Here, the being-historical Manichaeism is revoked, the distinction between "beyng" and "beings" is no longer a choice, and
technology as the "enemy" disappears, although the philosopher
does still speak of its "conversion" (*Verwindung*).[23]

A further example of what I am calling "being-historical
Manichaeism" is provided by a note from *Überlegungen* IX composed sometime around 1938. Heidegger remarks that while
"the Second World War occasionally" shifts "into the purview
of humans," it nevertheless seems "at other times as though the
authentic decision" can "not be counted upon." For such a decision
would mean "in no case: war or peace, democracy or authority,
Bolshevism or Christian culture—but instead either: *meditation*
[Besinnung] and the quest for an inceptual appropriation by
beyng or the *madness* of a final humanification [*Vermenschung*] of
an uprooted humanity."[24] Indeed, the human is most likely not

only "incapable of decision" but now "without need of decision." For "human contentment" in its "enjoyment (wherein mediocrity and violence go agreeably together)" increasingly escalates "into the gigantic." A more extreme either-or can scarcely be thought. It unfolds between a thinking of the freedom of Da-sein dwelling in "beyng," and the merely vegetative wasting away of a creature utterly integrated into the functioning of modern society, i.e., integrated into "beings."[25] Such a choice can only be a violent decision. Whoever ignores this decision falls victim to the "madness."

There is no narrative without leading and supporting roles for the actors. We have already heard that Heidegger speaks of "people and race," a formulation that he suppressed in the lecture courses prior to 1933. Even before this, though, we find in a manuscript, seemingly from out of the blue, the assertion: "The German alone can newly and originally poetize and say being— he alone will conquer anew the essence of θεωρία and finally produce *the logic*."[26] The narrative has at its beginning two leading actors: "the Greeks" and "the Germans," each time embodying, in a chiasmic manner, both beginning and end. "The Greeks" have marked "the beginning of Western philosophy." When this beginning goes over into its end, they themselves have a stake in this (in a way and manner we cannot further develop here). "The Germans," on the other hand, find themselves at the place where this end occurs, in that it arrives in the "West" (*Abendland*). But an end can take place in history only where a beginning occurs.

While all thinking is caught up in this end, it is "German thinking" as such that welcomes it. Indeed, as the Germans begin to discern this beginning by the Greeks, they become the ones capable of repeating it *otherwise*. What Heidegger expects of the Germans is at first a purely philosophical undertaking, to actualize anew the "essence of θεωρία" and produce "*the logic*"—i.e., another θεωρία and a logic different from the previous modern ones—projects the National Socialists certainly would have held for abstruse, had they had any interest in them whatsoever. For the sake of realizing this project, however, the end would first have to be prepared: "The greatness of the downfall [*Untergangs*] would be achieved—not as something worthless—rather as a seizing of and persisting in the most inner and extreme mission of the Germans," a statement that comes as the conclusion to the above remark concerning the demolition of philosophy. The "downfall" is the end indicative of the "mission of the Germans." It is the form of "demolition" that the end would knowingly actualize—and not simply allow to happen. Later, Heidegger will repeatedly return to this "mission" of "downfall."

Heidegger now saw the landscape of his thinking before him. The Greeks : the first beginning :: the Germans : the other beginning. Henceforth all that the Middle Ages, modernity, and contemporary times had brought forth would be enlisted into this relationship. And all that had appeared on the stage of history would be attributed to distinct protagonists. At first there were the "Romans," then the "Christians," and among these above all the "Jesuits," but also the "Protestants" and "Catholics," then the "Russians" or "the Russian" (*Russentum*), "the Chinese" (*Chinesentum*), the "English," the "French," the "Americans" or "Americanism," the "Europeans," the "Asians." All these collectives were localized within the relation of the first to the other beginning. And the "Jews" were added to this.

For us today, the use of such collective concepts has become problematic. To condemn them for Heidegger's time, however, is anachronistic.[27] It was common. Thus Hermann Cohen in his essay "Germanism and Judaism" ("Deutschtum und Judentum") from 1915 expresses himself in a way scarcely different from Heidegger's years later. As the Germans generally ascribed characteristics to the Jews, so do the Jews to the Germans.[28] The end of the Third Reich was the end of such collective concepts—and thereby the end of that Heideggerian narrative relying upon a polarity between "the Germans" and "the Greeks."

All that connected Heidegger to National Socialism stems from this narrative of the "first beginning" with the Greeks and an "other beginning" with the Germans. On the basis of this story, Heidegger embraces the "National Socialist revolution" and places himself in its service.[29] He connects a "spiritual National Socialism" to this, which he distinguished early on from a "*vulgar National Socialism*."[30] To the very end, up to the "capitulation," and despite all philosophical distancing, it was to this "spiritual National Socialism" that Heidegger remained loyal.[31] Heidegger's thinking was connected with National Socialism not "directly" but "indirectly"—according to Heidegger—since they both pressed "at the same time, in different ways, for a decision about the essence and definition of the Germans and with that the destiny of the West." For Heidegger, the revolution was from the very beginning precisely this: the mission of "the Germans" for a turning of the "destiny of the West."[32] It was difficult for Heidegger to part from such views, and only slowly did he find a thinking freed from the dream of a world-historical German revolution.

At the same time, however, it was this narrative that allowed Heidegger to position himself far from *actual* National Socialism. By the end of the 1930s his criticisms of National Socialism grow increasingly harsh, targeting its absolutizing of the race-concept, its biologism in general, its technologization of the country, its imperialism, and finally even its nationalism. Yet the fact that Heidegger could transform this critique into the philosophical thought of a text like "The Overcoming of Metaphysics" (1939), i.e., into the idea that an overcoming of National Socialism would be the ultimate—necessary—configuration of Western metaphysics, was itself already a result of this narrative's productivity.[33] What thus came about was a shift in Heidegger's relation to National Socialism: after the first phase of his entry into National Socialism, a phase tied to the hope for an immediate revolutionary realization of the "other beginning" and one that Heidegger establishes in a note as dating from "the years 1930–34," there follows a second phase, one concerned with "the necessity of its [National Socialism's] affirmation and indeed for *intellectual* reasons [denkerischen *Gründen*]," a phase that views National Socialism as a period of history, entirely fallen prey to "machination," but nevertheless necessary for the "overcoming of metaphysics" (another formulation of the "other beginning").[34]

How the Jews emerge in this being-historical topography is a question that until now could not be answered.

TYPES OF BEING-HISTORICAL ANTI-SEMITISM

Anti-Semitism *as such* is at the center of its most divergent forms. In regard to Heidegger, one finds in the *Black Notebooks* three remarks indicative of three different, internally coherent, types of being-historical anti-Semitism. The concept of a being-historical anti-Semitism should in no way imply that we are dealing with a particularly elaborate or refined anti-Semitism. In principle, Heidegger draws upon specific well-known forms. Nevertheless he interprets them philosophically, i.e., being-historically. The three types of this anti-Semitism become apparent in the following remarks:

1. The reason for Judaism's temporary increase in power, however, is that the metaphysics of the West, particularly in its modern development, provided the starting point for the spread of a rather empty rationality and calculative ability, which, in these ways, procured accommodation for itself in "spirit," without ever being able to grasp the concealed regions of decision on their own terms. The more original and inceptual these future decisions and questions become, the more inaccessible do they remain for this "race." (In this way, Husserl's step toward a phenomenological observation distinct from both psychological explanation and the historical accounting of opinions is of lasting importance—and nevertheless

nowhere does it extend to the region of essential decisions, but instead everywhere presupposes the historical tradition of philosophy; the necessary consequence of which shows itself at once in the acquiescing to neo-Kantian transcendental philosophy, which ultimately made an advance into Hegelianism in the formal sense inevitable. My "attack" against Husserl is not directed at him alone and is on the whole nonessential—the attack is against the neglect of the question of being, i.e., against the essence of metaphysics as such, on the basis of which the machination of beings is able to determine history. The attack grounds a historical moment of the highest decision between the precedence of beings and the grounding of the truth of beyng.)[1]

2. *With their marked gift for calculation,* the Jews "live" according to the principle of race, and indeed have done so for the longest time, for which reason they themselves most vigorously resist its unrestricted application. The arranging of racial breeding stems not from life itself, but rather from the overpowering of life by machination. What these pursue with such planning is a *complete deracination* of the peoples by harnessing them in a uniformly fabricated and sleek [*gleichgebaute und gleichschnittige*] arrangement of all beings. Deracination goes together with the self-alienation of the peoples—to the detriment of history, that is, to the detriment of the regions of decision for beyng.[2]

3. Even the thought of an agreement with England, in the sense of an allocation of imperialist "jurisdictions," does not get at the essence of the historical process which England plays out to the end from within Americanism and Bolshevism, and this means at the same time also from within world Judaism. The question concerning the role of *world Judaism* is not a racial one, but rather the metaphysical question concerning the kind of humanity which, *utterly unattached,* can take over the uprooting of all beings from being as its world-historical "task."[3]

CITATION 1

In the second half of the 1930s, sometime around 1937, in *Überlegungen* VIII, the Jews or Judaism expressly surface for the first time as actors in the being-historical narrative.[4] One "of the most hidden forms of the *gigantic* and perhaps the oldest" would be "the tenacious skillfulness at calculating and trafficking and intermixing, whereby the worldlessness of Judaism is grounded."[5] For Heidegger at this time, the "gigantic" is one of the forms of "machination," i.e., of the self-totalizing rationalizing and technologizing of the world. This development calls for a definite form of thinking, which he recognizes in the "skillfulness at calculating," i.e., in the "calculative ability," of the Jews.

This peculiar notion requires a more precise interpretation. For Heidegger does not proclaim that this "worldlessness" would be, so to speak, a natural characteristic of Judaism.[6] Rather, he thinks that it is first "grounded" through the "tenacious skillfulness at calculating." This "skillfulness," however, would be "one of the most hidden forms of the *gigantic*," i.e., of "machination." The origin of the worldlessness of Judaism is thus machination, which brings calculation to power as a world-defining activity. That machination requires and grounds the worldlessness of humans is a well-known thought from the repertoire of Heidegger's critique of technology; that this grounds the "worldlessness of Judaism" is a problematic narrowing of the point.

Accordingly Heidegger appears to take a quite banal anti-Semitic ascription (a "marked gift for calculation") and give it a being-historical transformation—and in this figure of thought his anti-Semitism is anchored. It is the figure of the "haggling Jew" (*Schacherjude*), who represents one of the most common figures of Judaism in all of anti-Semitism.[7] Since the twelfth century in the Christian West, the collecting of interest was forbidden, though the Jews were expressly excused from this by papal decree. Thus they were the sole group in society that was allowed to lend gold. At the same time, they were prohibited from taking up certain skilled trades. This was the historical situation in which "the Jew" immediately (i.e., without pursuing a "reputable profession") became bound up with money. Originally, *schachern* means in Yiddish "to pursue commerce."

Sociologically, the association of Judaism and money already begins to take hold in that provincial-rural way of life—as in Heidegger's hometown of Meßkirch—where the peasants and laborers earn their money "by the sweat of their brow," while Jews, for special reasons or those just mentioned, generate their income otherwise.[8] From here, the association returns in myriad attributions. One of these concerns a "world Judaism" that seizes world mastery through the control of national economies and other instruments (this pertains to the so-called *Protocols of the Elders of Zion*, which we will take up shortly in greater detail since Heidegger himself very probably refers to these). Another concerns the Jew's alleged metaphysical-religious attitude of "Mammonism," a concept of Georg Simmel's, which critically caricatures the idolization of money.[9] A further variant takes aim at calculation in general.

Heidegger quite generally connects calculation with rationality. With this he can classify his previous teacher Edmund Husserl within a history whereby "Judaism's temporary increase in power" damns the "metaphysics of the West, particularly in its modern development," to decisionlessness. Heidegger speaks of an "attack" on Husserl, though he instantly qualifies this. It would be "on the whole nonessential." Indeed, the qualification remains implausible against the background of the initial classification. Husserl is inscribed within a history of "empty rationality and calculative ability" on the basis of his belonging to a "'race.'" Surely one cannot overlook that Heidegger sets this concept off in quotation marks, but however one interprets this, it cannot mitigate the general direction of Heidegger's thought.

Problematic in Heidegger's utterance is not only the thought that Husserl's belonging to Judaism would be the reason that his phenomenology "nowhere" reaches into "the region of essential decisions." Beyond this, even after the war, Heidegger's frequently delivered critique of "calculative thinking," which is to be distinguished from "meditative thinking" and which, unlike the latter, can never find its way to a "rootedness" (*Bodenständigkeit*), acquires a rather bad taste.[10] For one of the counterconcepts to a "rootedness" in the "homeland" is that very "worldlessness" which, according to Heidegger—as consequence of "machination"—characterizes Judaism.[11] Would rationality as such then be a being-historical invention of the Jews—or does Heidegger rather grasp Judaism as a form in which "machination" actualizes itself?

Whatever the answer may turn out to be, it is erroneous to relate the "skillfulness at calculating" solely to the philosophy of modernity. Certainly one could say that mathematics attained a new significance in the technological applications and burgeoning natural science of the sixteenth and seventeenth centuries. But it must be clear that the *mathesis*, even in the mathematical sense, had its origin in Greek thinking.[12] This pertains to Heidegger's narrative of a being-historical relationship between the Greeks and the Germans, for in it there is simply no place for the Pythagoreans, for Plato's relation to them or for his introduction of mathematics particularly in the *Timaeus*, for Euclid and his *Elements*, not to mention for the Egyptians from whom the Greeks learned mathematics (even if interpreting it differently).

One type of anti-Semitism in Heidegger ascribes to the Jews a "skillfulness at calculating and trafficking and intermixing," which philosophically he interprets in an alarmingly broad manner. The Jew appears as the worldless, calculating subject, dominated by machination, which is supposed to have calculatingly "procured accommodation for itself in 'spirit.'" In this sense, then, precisely this "accommodation" would count as the target of Heidegger's "'attack.'"[13]

CITATION 2

In the first of the citations above, Heidegger indirectly explains Husserl's phenomenology in terms of the character of a "'race.'" The quotation marks should signal a certain distance. And, indeed, Heidegger is opposed to the "race thinking" of National Socialism. "All race thinking" would be "modern," would move "along the route of conceiving the human as subject."[14] Inevitably, Heidegger thus ascribes "race thinking" to the being of modernity (*Neuzeit*), to "machination." Race thinking is a "*consequence* of machination."[15]

It is thus clear that Heidegger wants nothing to do with race thinking. But this in no way means that he doubts the givenness of "race." "Race" would be "*one* necessary and indirectly telling condition of historical Dasein (throwness [*Geworfenheit*])." In race thinking this is "falsified into the sole and sufficient" condition. "*One* condition" is "raised to the unconditional."[16] Accordingly, Heidegger's distance from race thinking pertains to the theoretical absolutization of *one* moment of throwness among other moments, but not to the view that "race" belongs to Dasein.

Nevertheless, Heidegger does not flesh out how he considers "race" to be "*one* . . . condition" of throwness. Attention to the corporeality of Dasein is almost always out of the question for him. Even a cultural connotation is improbable here, since he generally interprets the concept of "culture" dismissively, if not disparagingly. Best would be to look into an ethnic importance for this. Accordingly "race" would be understood as a belonging to a people. But with this, the question of the meaning of "race" is merely repeated in a different context. What does "belonging to a people" mean beyond belonging to a linguistic community (and in this latter respect, the Jews would most assuredly be the better Germans)? The question of "race" in Heidegger will be elucidated in what follows. But even if Heidegger does not adopt the race thinking of machination, one can still reconstruct a convergence with the ideology of National Socialism.

The philosopher explains on the one hand that "race thinking" is a "consequence of machination." On the other hand, he holds that *"with their marked gift for calculation,* the Jews 'live' according to the principle of race, and indeed have done so for the longest time." How do these statements relate to each other? Must one consequence not be that "machination" and the "gift for calculation" belong together? It appears so. Nevertheless, the clarification of this issue requires some prudence, for the question concerns an element of being-historical anti-Semitism.

The "arranging of racial breeding stems not from life itself," Heidegger holds. "'Life'" thus occurs without organizing itself for the formation and ennoblement of races. With this thought, Heidegger does not mean to meddle in matters of biology. Rather he wants to say that the everyday dealings of humans are not concerned with the "keeping pure" of a "race." It thus requires an "arranging"—i.e., it requires machination, the origin of every "arranging"—for "'life'" to be organized in this way. On the one hand, Heidegger found this organization among the National Socialists. On the other hand, he also saw it with the Jews, who "'live' in accordance with the principle of race, and indeed have done so for the longest time," which can only mean that they were the first to realize a "distinctive feature" of machination, the "arranging of racial breeding." According to Heidegger, it was the Jews who took on a pioneering role in the "arranging of racial breeding," i.e., in the machinational organization of race.[17]

The background for this utterance is provided by, among other things, the Nuremberg racial laws, which were unanimously adopted by the Reichstag on September 15, 1935. A "Law for the Protection of German Blood and German Honor" as well as a "Law for the Protection of the Healthy Inheritance of the German People (Marriage Health Law)" used various criteria to discriminate among Jews, Gypsies, blacks, and half-breeds (incidentally, also women in general, even German women). Generally speaking, it was supposed to guarantee a division of the races by means of which "German blood" could be kept pure, i.e., unmixed.

Nevertheless, Heidegger does not merely say that the Jews would "'live' according to the principle of race, and indeed have done so for the longest time," for his proclamation continues: "for which reason they themselves most vigorously resist its unrestricted application." What is an "unrestricted application" of the "principle of race"? And what is the connection between one's own "application" of such a principle and the fight against its unrestrictedness that follows from this? Can Heidegger mean by this the Nuremberg laws?

The dating of the remark suggests that it was composed shortly before the outbreak of the Second World War. The November pogroms of 1938 are in the past. On November 10 of that year in Freiburg the synagogue near the university was burned down.[18] Even on November 9, Kristallnacht, Heidegger held a session of his seminar on Nietzsche's second "Unfashionable Observation."[19] Is it possible that when Heidegger wrote "the unrestricted application" of the "principle of race," he meant the violence that the Jews had to suffer?

This casts a peculiar light on the idea that the Jews would be the first who "lived" in accordance with the principle of race. The National Socialists make "unrestricted" application of that which the Jews practiced long before them. Further still: the explanation within the very title of the Nuremberg laws, i.e., that they would serve "*for the Protection* of German Blood," presupposes the danger of a contagious disease or a strategically acting assailant. The "unrestricted application" of the "principle of race" would then be a mere defensive measure within a conflict.

Nevertheless—and this is what is essential in all this—the invention of "race thinking" is being-historically contextualized. It would be a "consequence of machination." If Heidegger holds the "skillfulness at calculating" to be Jewish, and as typically modern, then all this taken together is now explained as an epiphenomenon of modern technology. For this reason he even writes "life" in quotation marks: "life" as absolute principle would be a consequence of the will to power, i.e., an inheritance from the last of the metaphysicians, Nietzsche. Heidegger inscribes the "racial thinking" of the Jews and the National Socialists into the history of being, into the history of machination. The enmity between the Jews and the National Socialists (Heidegger guards himself here from speaking of the Germans) results from a being-historical competition—and it is particularly problematic that the instigation of this inevitable conflict is assigned rather to the Jews.

At this point it must be emphasized that Heidegger attempted to conceive the "machinational" conflict between the Jews and the National Socialists in neutral terms. He remarks at one point that we should "not be too loudly incensed over the psychoanalysis of the Jew 'Freud,'" especially "if and so long as one *generally* cannot 'think' about everything and everyone" otherwise than in such a manner whereby "everything is regarded as an 'expression' of 'life.'"[20] With this, Heidegger criticizes even the "Aryan variants of the basic doctrine of psychoanalysis."[21] The philosopher speaks of "Jewish 'psychoanalysis'" as though this theory were in principle Jewish, a possible interpretation familiar since the birth of psychoanalysis and one that, by the time of National Socialism, had become an anti-Semitic stereotype.[22]

What "machination" secretly pursues with this covert competition is—so Heidegger—a *complete deracination of the peoples.* This goes along with a "self-alienation of the peoples—to the detriment of history, that is, to the detriment of the regions of decision for beyng." If we emphasized above that Heidegger in no way rejects the thought of race itself, only its absolutization, then this statement is the starkest proof of that. For if race, according to Heidegger, is a moment of "thrownness," and this, however, as the finitude of Dasein, is something like the condition of historicality, then a "complete deracination of the peoples" is consequently "to the detriment of history." To be sure, it is still not explained how two enemies who pursue the "principle of race" could nevertheless contribute to a "complete deracination."

This second type of anti-Semitism in Heidegger can thus be characterized as "racial" or "racist." To be sure, Heidegger rejects "race thinking." Nevertheless he assumes a particular significance of race for "thrownness," and this means a particular significance of race for historicality. Heidegger is thus by no means of the view that there would be a superiority of the Aryans. Nevertheless—and this is a quite troubling "nevertheless"—he is of the view that the battle between the Jews and the National Socialists is a battle for the sake of history, and one that is conducted from racial motives.

CITATION 3

In his *Philosophical Autobiography,* Karl Jaspers writes of Heidegger: "I spoke about the Jewish question, about the evil irrationality of the Elders of Zion, to which he replied: 'There truly is a dangerous international band of Jews.'"[23] The *Protocols of the*

Elders of Zion arose in the horizon of the Dreyfus affair, which played itself out in the Paris of the 1890s; the context of the affair reaches deep into the czarist politics of the time.[24] It also includes the spread of anti-Semitic novels as well as a growth in the significance of Zionism, which was especially propelled forward since 1860 by the Alliance Israélite Universelle and since 1897 by the Zionist World Organization. The inaugural meeting of the latter in Basel was the fictional origin of the *Protocols*. Their striking proliferation began after the First World War. In Germany they appeared for the first time in 1920.

The effect of the *Protocols* was astonishing, even from today's point of view. Technically speaking, the book was not a forgery, but rather a complete fiction since no original exists.[25] The *Protocols* became the first source of modern anti-Semitism. Hitler has been characterized as an early "student of the elders of Zion," meaning that he found incitements there for working out a totalitarian racial politics.[26] Alfred Rosenberg commented on the *Protocols*. Hannah Arendt noted that "the masses were not so frightened by Jewish world rule as they were interested in how it could be done, that the popularity of the *Protocols* was based on admiration and eagerness to learn rather than on hatred."[27] Thus for her the methods of the National Socialists were clear: "The Nazis started with the fiction of a conspiracy and modeled themselves, more or less consciously, after the example of the secret society of the Elders of Zion."[28] The *Protocols* are the proof of the competition between the Jews and the National Socialists, as mentioned above, a competition that Heidegger obviously accepts.

In the *Protocols of the Elders of Zion* one finds many types of the anti-Semitic phantasmagoria. The first is that of a secret organization that spins its webs at the level of global decisions. All possible means are deployed on its behalf: politics, finance, culture, communism, the press, everything gets subverted, everywhere

TYPES OF BEING-HISTORICAL ANTI-SEMITISM // 29

unrest is fomented. Even philosophy is deployed. Thus the *Protocols* say at one point: "Do not believe that our proclamations would be only empty words. Look at the success of the teachings of Darwin, Marx, and Nietzsche as disseminated by us. Their destructive effect on non-Jewish heads should at least be clear to us."[29] The philosophers—marionettes of "world Judaism."

More than these characteristic remarks, another statement could have had an effect on Heidegger. Under the heading "The Repression of the Resistance of Non-Jews through Wars and a Universal World War," it says: "As soon as a non-Jewish state hazards to resist us, we must be in the position to occasion its neighbors to go to war against it. But if the neighbors seek to make common cause with it and proceed against us, then we must unleash world war."[30] This gets directly to the point of the competition assumed by Heidegger. Did the National Socialists not hazard to proceed against "world Judaism"? And did the latter not succeed in the perfect counterstrike?

Various speeches show that Hitler understood how to use the *Protocols* for propaganda and just how he did so. In a speech that he gave in Berlin-Siemensstadt on November 10, 1933, he spoke of "the struggle between peoples" as "fostered" by "folk with definite interests to promote." It is "an uprooted international clique" that "incites the peoples one against another." Here we are dealing with "folk who are at home everywhere and nowhere: they have no soil of their own on which they have grown up: to-day they are living in Berlin, to-morrow they may be in Brussels, the day after in Paris, and then again in Prague or Vienna or London." They are such that "everywhere they feel themselves at home." They are "international elements" because "everywhere they can carry on their business." But "the people," i.e., the Germans, "cannot follow them," for "the people is chained to its soil, is tied to its homeland, tied to the possibilities of life of its State, its nation."[31] Or in that speech in the Reichstag on January 30,

1939, in which he "prophesied": "Once again I will be a prophet: should the international Judaism of finance succeed, both within and beyond Europe, in plunging the peoples into yet another world war, then the result will not be a Bolshevization of the earth and the victory of Judaism, but the annihilation of the Jewish race in Europe."[32] Stereotypes of anti-Semitism from the *Protocols*.

Heidegger had an ear for Hitler's speeches. In any case, he contemplates to what extent the English also take on the role of "world Judaism" in "Americanism and Bolshevism."[33] Heidegger wants to understand this not as a "racial" phenomenon, but rather as a "metaphysical" one. The English would be "the kind of humanity which, *utterly unattached*, can take over the uprooting of all beings from being as its world-historical 'task.'" If it is the case that Heidegger accepts a competition between the National Socialists and Jews, one roused and conducted by machination, then it now becomes clearer which role is represented by Judaism in this battle. Machination can pursue the "complete deracination of the peoples" because the Jews *"utterly unattached,"* strive for "the uprooting of all beings."

With this widespread tendency to ascribe to the Jews a homeless, i.e., cosmopolitan, way of life, there arises the notion of an enemy who conducts an inconceivable war on an international level.[34] Thus Heidegger says at one time:

> World Judaism, spurred on by the emigrants let out of Germany, is everywhere elusive. In all the unfurling of its power, it need nowhere engage in military actions, whereas it remains for us to sacrifice the best blood of the best of our own people.[35]

At first glance, the sentence appears quite simple to interpret. But its context makes an interpretation difficult. Fairness is an indispensable presupposition of interpretation. Thus I must briefly enter into the context.

The entire *Überlegung* bears the heading "At the start of the third year of planetary war." Heidegger assembles ten statements that present the current state of the war. Before this we read: "Insofar as one thinks only historiologically and not historically and still does not include planetarism in the transformation of history, but instead employs this planetarism only geographically at best and as a frame for 'historiological' incidents, insofar as one values only 'facts' that are always only half-truths and thus erroneous, the following assessments are applicable." As the ninth point there appears the above-cited statement about "world Judaism."

There are two possibilities for interpreting the "insofar" here: (1) as a restriction; (2) as a concession. As a restriction, it could mean: what follows is not meant seriously, it is solely an overview that I, Heidegger, take to be entirely inapplicable. As a concession it could mean: what follows is written for those who are desperately interested in "'historiological'" "'facts.'" Even this point of view should be legitimate here.

I have decided upon the second possibility. I admit that it contradicts many other comparable passages in the *Black Notebooks*. Heidegger despises "'historiological' incidents" most of all. But here he appears to consider that even these have a specific significance. Beneath the superficies of "obliquely" formulated texts, one recognizes Heidegger's actual intention, i.e., his worry over the victory of the armed forces.

The advantage of "world Judaism" in the battle against "us" occasioned by machination consists in the ability to guide the fates from somewhere or other, while remaining "everywhere elusive." Further, "world Judaism"—as proclaimed in the *Protocols*—is evidently able to set armies in motion without ever committing itself. The sacrifice lies on "our" side. How the battle will conclude through this "unfurling of power" is clear. Particularly grave is the remark that "world Judaism" would be "spurred on by the emigrants let out of Germany." Is Heidegger thinking of Thomas Mann, who beginning in October 1941 appealed to the "German listener" in his transmitted addresses from the BBC in London? Or does he think of the refugees more generally and, among them, of the Jews? To be sure, Heidegger in no way makes a case that they should *not* have been "let out," but the suggestion is not far.

The sacrifice of the "best blood of the best of our own people"—without doubt, in these words Heidegger also addresses the fate of his two sons. If in this regard he abandons his otherwise rather consistently maintained neutrality, we can assume an intimate involvement in the matter. Heidegger was strongly partisan on the question of the war and the sacrifice of the German soldiers—and he could not eschew lending his partisanship a being-historical note.[36]

"World Judaism" does not master history—which is unconditionally controlled by machination—but among the powers dominated by technology it appears to be the first. Thus the "imperialist-militaristic and the humanist-pacifist ways of thinking"—i.e., the ways of thinking of the totalitarian states (the German Reich, Italy, and the Soviet Union) as well as of the Western democracies—would be "offshoots of 'metaphysics.'" As such, they appear to be infiltrated by "world Judaism." For Heidegger continues:

> Thus both [of these ways of thinking] are able to serve "international Judaism," the one as a means for calling out and bringing about the other—this machinational "history"-making traps all players equally in its nets.[37]

"World Judaism" would thus have the power to play the states off against each other—specifically those that find themselves at war—in that it would be "served" by their "ways of thinking." It is not obvious whether Heidegger subsumes "international

Judaism" under the previously named ways of thinking within "this machinational 'history'-making" or whether he reserves this "history"-making for "international Judaism" alone. In any event, the thought shows how Heidegger wavered in his interpretation of the relation between "world Judaism" and machination. On the one hand he attributed to "world Judaism" a privileged place as the internationally acting representative of technology. On the other hand, this would all belong to the same history. In this "battle," the success of those who proclaim and achieve "world domination" is "no less irrelevant than the fate of those most ground down." All would still be "at the level of metaphysics" and would thus remain "excluded from anything different." The Jews would be just a further configuration of the metaphysical topology.

With this, it appears that Heidegger was clear about the consequences of the war, particularly for the Jews. In the manuscript on the *Geschichte des Seyns* (History of Beyng), in those passages singular in content and concerning the being-historical dimension of "power," Heidegger speaks of the "planetary master criminals of the most modern modernity"—and means without doubt the prime rulers of the totalitarian states.[38] "The question remains," however, "what is the basis for the peculiar predetermination of Jewry [*eigentümliche Vorbestimmung der Judenschaft*] for planetary criminality."[39] At first, this statement suggests a straightforward understanding: Heidegger asks what could have propelled the Jews into this "peculiar predetermination" of becoming the victims of "planetary master criminals."

Admittedly, though, the statement does not preclude Heidegger from seeing the "peculiar predetermination of Jewry" not as becoming the victims of those criminals, but rather as being those criminals themselves.[40] This interpretation would also fit with Heidegger's utterances concerning the power of "world Judaism." Certainly for Heidegger, the "planetary master criminals" included Stalin and Hitler, but we cannot rule out that along with Hitler and Stalin, this characterization encompassed "Jewry" as well. However we might read the sentence, the formulation "*peculiar* [*eigen*-tümliche, as related to Er-*eignis*] predetermination" (my italics) attests to the being-historical character of this thinking about the Jews.

Similar to the "skillfulness at calculating" that is attributed to the Jews, this third type of anti-Semitism in Heidegger, oriented around the *Protocols of the Elders of Zion*, is difficult to delimit. The lecture course from the summer of 1942 on Hölderlin's "Ister" hymn shows this. Here Heidegger sees the Germans threatened more than ever by "Americanism," i.e., by the "unhistorical." This threat, however, comes not from without but from within. The philosopher could not understand why the Germans were not in a position to recognize what is their "own" in the relationship between "poetizing and thinking" as outlined by him. Instead of this, they went along with the global "total mobilization," indeed, they even became its leading exponents. Hidden behind "Americanism," was there not the "everywhere elusive" world Judaism?

In general, the opposite of everything Heidegger sought to save philosophically—"rootedness," "homeland," what is "one's own," the "earth," the "gods," "poetry," etc.—appears to be transposable onto "world Judaism." Consequently this receives a kind of paradigmatic status. When Rabbi Joachim Prinz proclaims (cited in note 34) that the "fate of the European metropolises in general" would be embodied in the "fate" of the Jews, then the Jew, who "has the 'nose' [*Riecher*]" for what is modern, would be the antagonist of Heideggerian thinking plain and simple.[41]

Note that what is anti-Semitic in this is not the identification of Judaism with an international lifestyle. Even Arendt conceded that the "lies about a Jewish world conspiracy" had "based themselves on the existing international interrelationship and interdependence of a Jewish people dispersed all over the world," i.e., in the Diaspora.[42] It is not anti-Semitic to see in this way of life an "uprooting." But it *is* anti-Semitic to assign to this way of life a concrete enmity against the "rootedness" of the Germans. If Heidegger, speaking to Jaspers, mentioned an "international band of Jews" (and there is no cause for believing Jaspers to be deceiving himself or falsely remembering), then he could indeed do so with a view to the Diaspora; but to characterize this band as "dangerous" betrays the anti-Semitic background.

And yet Heidegger appears to evade such a reproach when he situates the conflict with "world Judaism" within machination. It functions as the being-historical movement in which the battle is carried out. Through this interpretation, Heidegger's anti-Semitism obtains its distinctive character. For in the battle between world Judaism and the National Socialists, Heidegger in no way would have welcomed a "'victory'" by the latter. Quite the contrary—since, according to Heidegger, this battle can only concern "sheer aimlessness."[43] The "authentic victory," by contrast, lies for him "where the rootless [*Bodenlose*]" excludes "itself," because it "does not venture beyng, but instead always only" calculates "with beings," and posits "its calculations as the actual." In this statement it is by no means obvious whether, in addition to Judaism, the "rootless" can also bear the character of "machination." Philosophically for Heidegger it was important to understand why "the Western" had not experienced itself "as history" and opened itself "for what comes [*ein Kommendes*]," "instead of—unwittingly throughout it all—imitating and exaggerating Americanism."[44] The West had fallen prey to machination; the task originating with the Greeks of founding a world in "thinking and poetizing" appeared lost. Why?

At last the difficulty of such a being-historical construction itself comes to light. In the battle of the National Socialists with the Jews as a "consequence of machination," there reigns an asymmetry worth considering. Heidegger remarks in many places that the National Socialists recklessly promoted the technologization and, in this respect, modernization of the country. Indeed the chief characteristic of the technological, of the "machinational," was the "rootless" (*Bodenlose*), the "worldless," which the philosopher likewise ascribed to Judaism. Were the National Socialists then actually Germans deceived by "machination," i.e., deceived by the Jews? In the light of this question the National Socialists become marionettes of the "everywhere elusive" power of the Jews. Do the *Protocols* not suggest the idea that National Socialism itself could have been the most malicious invention of the Jews? In any event, the "self-exclusion" of the "rootless"—which Heidegger characterized as the "authentic victory"—would be the collapse of both "machination" *and* Judaism.

With this, the concept of machination itself falls into a crisis. To be sure, Heidegger emphasizes that the word "machination" names "an essencing of *being*" (*ein Wesen des* Seins) and "not somehow the comportment and demeanor of a particular being named 'the human'"; consequently "*the latter* machination," i.e., that of the "human," is "thought of as at most a distant consequence of the beyng-historical one." Is not "world Judaism" or "Americanism" precisely the model for such an "essence of being"?[45] The concept of machination could contain ideological moments that are not far from those that are ideologically ascribed to "world Judaism"—without, however, being reducible to these moments.[46] The thought that machination would pursue a military conflict between Jews and National Socialists, which nonetheless would only circle about in "aimlessness," cannot wipe away the impression at this point of an anti-Semitic influence of the *Protocols* upon Heidegger's thinking. When Heidegger writes that in Americanism, "nihilism" reaches "its pinnacle," then no possible resolution of that conflict can hinder this any longer.[47]

This delineates the actual problem with a being-historical anti-Semitism. If certain elements of the being-historical narrative are to retain a determinate role from the outset—if, for example, "Americanism" could not have come about otherwise than as the "organizing of the nonessence of machination," if then "everything horrible" is supposed to lie "in Americanism,"[48] precisely because "Americanism" is simply incapable of a "beginning," because it does not know the "origin," because it is the offspring of an England that pursues its "gigantic business" (cf. note 33)—then is the history of being itself not anti-Semitic?

THE BEING-HISTORICAL
CONCEPT OF "RACE"

Heidegger's conception of race is ambivalent. Clearly the concept was kept out of his philosophical texts prior to 1933. Before 1933, the philosopher generally kept silent about his political sympathies for the National Socialists. When we take into account his publications and lectures, it becomes difficult to discern where he could have interested himself philosophically in something like "race."

Regarding the concept of "race," it can generally be said that its provenance is actually not to be found in biology. It "relates above all to the kinds of animals that have been newly produced by humans through domestication and breeding."[1] When Plato carries over the breeding of dogs, birds, and horses to humans in his *Republic* (459b), he is admittedly less concerned with new production than with eugenic ennoblement. Plato's great student in the nineteenth century, Nietzsche, probably has such ideas in mind when he notes in *Daybreak* that "the Greeks" offer us "the model of a race and culture that have become pure."[2] Nevertheless even Nietzsche's relation to the concept of race is anything but univocal, as shown by the fact that he regards the "Greeks" as the "model" for a "pure *European* race and culture."[3]

Heidegger sees the problematic status of "race" in Nietzsche.

He could also see how the application of the concept of race in Ernst Jünger's *Der Arbeiter* (The Worker) brought with it complications. Jünger speaks of the "race of the worker," thus of a "new race," which mobilizes the world.[4] Indeed, Jünger adds that this "race within the landscape of work" would have "nothing to do with the biological concept of race."[5] It is telling that the concept of race as found in contemporary discourses forces its way into the text. Jünger wanted to enter into these discussions, without thereby giving himself entirely over to them. The actuality of the concept of "race" was recognized by Jünger.

This would also have to be Heidegger's strategy. He was prepared to take up the dominant discourse so as to set himself apart from it at the same time, a movement of thought that Heidegger often performed around 1933. In his lecture course of summer 1934, *Logic as the Question concerning the Essence of Language,* he comes to speak about "race." The concept would mean "*not only* that which is racial [*Rassisches*], as in the bloodline [*Blutmäßige*] in the sense of heredity, of hereditary blood connection, and of the drive to live," but also "at the same time, often that which is racy [*das Rassige*]." "Racial in the first sense does not by a long shot need to be racy"; instead "it can rather be very drab [*unrassig*]."[6] Heidegger's dealings with the concept of "race" appear akin to Jünger's. It is altered into his own language and integrated into it. There is, however, a decisive difference.

Heidegger does not doubt the biological significance of the concept. "Race" is "*not only* that which is racial as in the bloodline."[7] That there is this "bloodline" is not put into question. Much more, the philosopher speaks in the same lecture course of the "voice of the blood" in its relation to the "fundamental attunement of the human."[8] For a moment, "blood" takes center stage. This is also seen in a sequence of concepts from the seminar on Hegel's *Philosophy of Right.* "*Care*" would have to be understood as "*truth* (nature—soil—blood—homeland—landscape—gods—death)"; a sequence of concepts that are not placed together accidentally.[9]

Just as Heidegger proceeds with the concept of race, namely, by acknowledging its positive significance in order then to restrict it (nevertheless in a seemingly obscure way, for what is "racy"?),[10] so too does he treat the ideologeme of "blood and soil."[11] "Blood and soil" are "indeed powerful and necessary, but they are *not sufficient* conditions for the Dasein of the people."[12] Like race, the blood is a "necessary" but not "sufficient condition." So too runs the formulation already mentioned in *Überlegungen* III: "*One* condition" is "raised to the unconditional."

So much appears clear, but the question remains as to what positive significance Heidegger sees in the necessary condition of race for historical Dasein. The reference he gives is restricted to "thrownness" and "blood." In a further statement from the first of the *Black Notebooks*, he speaks of the "power of 'race' (the native)."[13] This "power," however, would not be developed. Instead a "short-sighted cluelessness" was bred. This omission of development pertains to "thrownness." What lies ready for further development here does not get actualized. Put in the language of *Being and Time*, it could be said that "thrownness" here lacks a "project."

A statement of Heidegger's corresponding to this idea links "project" with the ideologeme of "blood and soil." The "project of being as time" would overcome "everything prior in being and thinking." It would concern not only an "idea," but a "mission," for the sake of not a "solution" but rather a "bonding." This "project" is not "converted into pure spirit," but rather first opens and binds "blood and soil to a preparedness for activity, to effectiveness, and to the *capacity for work*."[14] Understood in this way, "blood and soil" appear as a thrownness that takes effect only in such a projection. The thrownness of "blood and soil" would then be "race" as a necessary condition, one that first receives its mission and its bond in the project—namely, a belonging to the "body of the people [*Volkskörper*] in the sense of the corporeal life," a belonging that first attains its authentic significance in this project.[15]

Thus the philosopher defines the "rootedness" that he repeatedly addressed as the attribute of a human who "coming from out of the soil, [is] nourished by this and stands upon it." That would be "the originary—that—which often undulates through my body and mood—as though I went across the fields at the plow, along lonely field paths through ripening grain, through the winds and fog, sun and snow, that which kept the blood of the mother and that of her ancestors circulating and undulating."[16] Race is one's belonging to a "body of the people" in the sense of the "blood of the mother" and "that of her ancestors." It is the "origin" in this sense.

Given Heidegger's concession of a legitimate use of the concept of race (something directly conveyed by his restriction of its use), we must pose the question as to whether he is not applying a rhetorical figure here that allows him in his dealings with the National Socialists to pursue his own ideas potentially critical of the regime. Without question, we cannot rule out that the philosopher may have wanted to keep suspicions at arm's length, when, in the academic meetings immediately after 1933— especially as rector of Freiburg University—he approached the National Socialists in the hopes of drawing them in his direction. It is also quite likely that he never agreed philosophically with National Socialism as it actually existed (and if so, then only within very narrow limits). Not without reason did he keep the *Black Notebooks* and the being-historical treatises hidden from publicity. To be sure, our concern here is not at all with this issue. Ours is much rather to show that Heidegger could definitely combine a being-historical anti-Semitism—including a being-historical concept of race—with a critical distance from actual National Socialism.

Already during the course of his rectorship, Heidegger attributed increasing importance to the supposed incapacity of the Germans to set in motion their "body of the people" in relations of "thrownness" and "projection." The "many who now" give speeches "'about' race and rootedness" would prove "by every word and in everything they do and fail to do . . . that they not only 'have' nothing of all that, but even less *are* racy [*rassig*] and autochthonous from the ground up."[17] As he did in other areas where the ideological motives proclaimed in the revolution of 1933 were concretely actualized, Heidegger the rector began quite quickly to strike critical notes also in regard to race. The revolution, in his eyes, did not live up to its potential. There was talk "'about' race and rootedness," belonging to a "body of the people" was emphasized, but no consequences were drawn from this. The project-character of race, namely, the "Western responsibility" of the Germans, this *"people of the earth,"* was simply not recognized.[18]

Along with disappointment over these missed revolutionary chances, an authentic philosophical reaction also followed: "All 'blood' and all 'race,' every 'people' [*Volkstum*]" is "in vain and a blind course of action, if this has not already" swung over "into a risking of being" and "as a risking" placed itself "freely before the lightning bolt," which would meet it there "where its numbness" would necessarily "disintegrate," "for the sake of making room for that truth of beyng, within which beyng" could first be "set in the work of beings."[19] The view has changed. Heidegger acknowledges more and more that the thrownness of race recedes before the "risk" of corresponding to the "truth of beyng."

The path that Heidegger set out upon in the late 1930s in regard to the concept of race is the same that he took in nearly all dimensions of his relations with National Socialism. The more he saw that the narrative of the "first" and "other beginning" had nothing to do with the "national revolution," the more clearly he recognized that actual National Socialism never had any interest in orienting itself on Hölderlin's poetry, the more he kept his philosophical distance from "race thinking."

"All race thinking" is "modern," it moves "along the lines of conceiving the human as subject." In "race thinking," the "subjectivism of modernity" is "consummated through the inclusion of corporeality in subjectivity and the complete grasping of subjectivity as the humanity of the human masses." "At the same time" there occurs an "unconditional empowering of machination."[20] Wherever the human with its body-soul-spirit-anthropology makes itself the foundation of being, a "*brutalitas* of being" is instated whereby the human turns itself "into a *factum brutum*" and "'grounds' its animality through the doctrine of race."[21] This thought, which Heidegger also stated publicly (in the Nietzsche lectures, for example), forms the core of the being-historical critique of race thinking. An apologetics that would like to recognize a thoroughgoing renunciation of the concept of "race" here simply goes astray.

This holds even when Heidegger distances himself ever further from actually existing National Socialism. "Indeed, one should not fall prey to the basic deception," he says at one point, "as though with this insight into the biological breeding conditions of the 'people,' an insight easily possible for anyone, something essential would be hit upon—whereas the predominance of this biological way of thinking, crude and contemporary by its very nature," precisely hinders "a meditation upon the fundamental conditions of being a people." The "knowing and even producing of these conditions" would have to be a "liberation from all calculation of utility . . . whether this be for private or common use."²² With this renunciation of the "insight into the biological breeding conditions of the 'people,'" Heidegger appears to call for something like an abolition of the Nuremberg racial laws. What a "people" is cannot be brought about by technological organization. At this time, the philosopher leads the genesis of a "people" back to "Da-sein" in an entirely nonbiological manner.²³

But now it seems advisable not to lose sight of the remark about the Jewish "gift for calculation." Must the needed "liberation from all calculation of utility" not awaken the impression that Heidegger wanted the Germans to free themselves from their epigonal role in relation to the "racial principle" of the Jews? Certainly not every criticism of calculative thinking can be led back to Heidegger's anti-Semitic invective that the Jews would be the avant-garde of racial politics. But here we also cannot let the being-historical-anti-Semitic contamination of Heideggerian thinking mentioned above simply go unremarked.

We must carefully consider how the being-historical interpretation of race belongs in the context of the self-unfolding narrative of the history of being more generally. One aspect of the criticism of "race thinking" repeats the criticism already mentioned of an erroneous absolutization of "race." It appears now as one moment of an inherent tendency within the "subjectivism of modernity" to posit the subject absolutely, along with its specific anthropology and organization. But this can in no way mean that Heidegger would have to distance himself from continuing to take race seriously as a historical phenomenon. On the contrary: the "unconditionality" of machination includes the absoluteness of "race thinking" so inescapably within it that only with this does race actually become relevant at all, namely, in its being-historical significance.

Now "world Judaism" must be presented as one of the leading

figures of machination. This results from its unconditionality. Since the Jews have lived "for the longest time in accordance with the principle of race," they have a privileged position in the play-space of the "subjectivism of modernity" as situated within the unconditionality of machination. At this point it becomes conceivable that Heidegger's statements about the Jews need not be bound up with an aggressive aversion to them. Taking into account the *Protocols of the Elders of Zion,* one can assume that in Heidegger's eyes the topography of the history of being made a recourse to the "unfurling power" of the Jews inevitable.

If the being-historical integration of race thinking into the subjectivism of modernity in no way makes the concept of race superfluous, then this already shows that the "deracination of the peoples" appears as a "self-alienation" for Heidegger. He still holds that race would be a necessary, even if not an absolute, condition of the body of the people. A later thought also accords with this. As Heidegger increasingly emphasized the being-historical significance of the Russians toward the end of the 1930s, he at one time posed the question "why the purifying and securing of the race should not one day be defined as having had as its consequence a great *mixing*: with the Slavs," with "the Russians—upon whom Bolshevism would have been forced and not something rooted in them."[24] In the "Russians" the philosopher saw a parallel to the Germans. Like the Germans, the Russians would be held in check by the unconditionality of machination. What here was National Socialism, there was Bolshevism. And the third figure of the "planetary master criminals" was "world Judaism."

Being-historical anti-Semitism consists in Heidegger thinking: the Jews, living "in accordance with the principle of race," in the "unconditionality" of "machination," this "*brutalitas* of being," interpret themselves in a manner founded precisely on this "principle of race," which surrenders them, "utterly unattached," to the pursuit of an "uprooting of beings" with the aim and intent of their "unfurling of power." World Judaism must have appeared to him as a people, or as a group within a people, who single-mindedly pursue no other aim than the putrefaction of all other peoples: a "race" that consciously pursues the "deracination of the peoples."

THE FOREIGN AND
THE FOREIGN

One of the most irritating thoughts in Heidegger's thinking at the end of the 1930s is that "machination" would pursue a "*complete deracination* of the peoples by harnessing them in a uniformly fabricated and sleek arrangement of all beings" and that thereby a "self-alienation of the peoples" would take effect "to the detriment of history." The problem in thinking the relation between race and people in Heidegger has already been addressed. The connection between "deracination" and "self-alienation of the peoples" suggests the assumption of a connection of some sort between race and what is proper (*Eigenen*) to a people; "of some sort" because Heidegger could never make the connection clear.

The proper, one's own, is distinguished from the foreign. We could then ask, how did Heidegger think the foreign? What is conspicuous is that at the start of the 1930s and across the further course of the decade a great amount of space is devoted to the word cluster around the term "foreign": "foreignness," "strangeness," "estranging," the "most strange," the "ever-strange" (*Fremdheit, Befremdlichkeit, Befremdung, das Befremdlichste, das Nur-befremdliche*). Heidegger is at pains to connect a philosophy of the foreign with the specific choreography of a revolution. At the moment when the customary breaks apart, everything should become other, and that means "foreign."

Heidegger's philosophical intention thus aims at a rather strange project: "To *goad* humanity through the entire foreignness and strangeness of the essence of being, with all the essentiality of it."[1] The "essence of being" is foreign. This foreignness apparently produces a certain comportment of refusal in humans, which necessitates "goading" them. This occurrence is supposed to take nothing from the essence of being, its "essentiality" is to be retained. The revolution must be radical.

The topography of being now becomes a unique landscape of the foreign. The question "why are there beings at all and not nothing?"—for Heidegger *the* question of metaphysics—becomes the "*approach* into what is estranging of the foreign, of the *Da*."[2] "Da-sein"—a foreign location. Philosophy has the task of opening this location. It "goes back into the concealed as the incomprehensible and estranging."[3]

In this landscape, particular thinkers come to embody the foreign. "Heraclitus—Kant—Hölderlin—Nietzsche" are "entirely foreign," and must be put back "into what is their great ownmost [*Eigenstes*]," so that "we with our half measures" do not make them "common."[4] Thinkers are—according to a saying of Socrates—the atopical, the placeless. They are the ones who "found [*stiften*] beyng and think the truth of beyng," who are "foreigners among beings and estranging to everyone."[5]

What matters is the "arrival of another truth," for the sake of an "assault by the fullness of the ever-strange."[6] This "other truth" cannot be accommodated within the customary, i.e., usual, conception of truth. The "assault by the fullness of the ever-strange" is the philosophically intensified understanding of revolution. In this, nothing more should remain of what Heidegger could only view as configurations of the end.

The "ever-strange" can be clarified philosophically only through the distinction between beings and being, i.e., through the splitting off of being from beings, a splitting off that is still termed the "ontological difference" at the beginning of the 1930s. Being itself is the fully other to beings. It is so much other that it must be thought as the not-being (*Nicht-Seiende*). This being (*Sein*) withdraws itself, is concealed, and can be experienced only as the "truth of beyng," in the sense of a concealment, of a withdrawal into particular and fundamental moods. Since it contains nothing known and usual, it can be characterized as the "ever-strange."

We can extend Heidegger's thought a bit further. We can pose a question concerning the atopography of the foreign, an atopography that could liberate the foreign and its place or placelessness from a boring dialectic of foreign and familiar.[7] In such a xenology, a philosophy of the foreign as the foreign of philosophy—i.e., as a thinking of the foreign that would not itself remain untouched by this—could perhaps develop. Heidegger's thinking of the foreign shows how extreme he thought the consequences of revolution to be and how radically he thereby destroyed every form of politics—even the Platonic. The revolution was for him a total being-historical upheaval, not only of the accustomed lifeworld, but also of philosophy, science, art, and religion. Clearly, the National Socialists could not have held something like this to be anything but the remote idea of a daydreamer. Heidegger well knew why he entrusted such ideas only to the *Black Notebooks*, why he—as he says—"kept them silent."[8]

Such questions of philosophy are certainly not unknown since the Neoplatonism of a Plotinus, since the mystical theology of a Pseudo-Dionysius, or since certain sermons of Meister Eckhart. Seen this way, Heidegger shows himself to belong to a particular tradition of thought that acknowledges the foreignness of philosophical truth and defends this against comfortable simplifications. All in all, we can say that behind the revolutionary pathos of Heidegger's style, for which the taste of the times is responsible, there stand enticing philosophical questions.

The authentic problem, however, begins somewhere else. Remarkably, Heidegger did not reserve the phenomenon of the foreign solely for being, but also acknowledged a foreignness of beings. Otherwise it cannot be understood why, in connection with the "radio apparatus," which had "already been talked up" to the "peasants," he comes to speak of "urban foreigners" who "increasingly flood the village."[9] Here foreignness obtains another meaning. It is experienced as something that endangers the presumed origin. "Technology and uprooting" form a unity in which technological devices destroy the original customs of life.[10]

Heidegger's dealings with foreigners become still more problematic when he inscribes them into the being-historical polarity of Germans and Greeks, of the "first" and the "other beginning" of philosophy. Here he avers a "hereditary defect of the Germans of looking toward the foreign." This defect would have to be "overcome" and one's "own taste" developed. It would be wrong "to emulate the other" and to put "every last thing on 'politics.'" For the more "what is one's ownmost" is taken as merely "what is one's own [das Seine] and something incomparable," the more easily does a people lose it.[11]

This "hereditary defect—the running-after-the-other and the aggrandization of the foreign because it is foreign" would have to be set aside.[12] On the whole, "the Germans tumble in the essential foreignness that modernity" has forced upon them. Therein would lie "the danger that they fall prey to the exclusive dominance of their own un-essence."[13] The "un-essence" is, on the one hand, the National Socialists serving "machination," and, on the other hand, it is that "hereditary defect" itself.

This leads to the dramatic-sounding question: *"What have the Germans stumbled into?"* They would always still be just where Hölderlin and Nietzsche found them. Thus the increasingly resigned suspicion that "perhaps" it would be the "essence of the

Germans" to "ever still and ever more unwittingly—aggrandize and imitate 'the foreign.'" "Perhaps" this abnegation of "essence" would come "from their *still* more fundamentally practiced 'Americanism,' and from their *still* more 'restlessly' executed 'Romanism.'" Then they would not be the "people" that "prepares for beyng the site of its truth."[14]

Otherwise stated: "Liberation" for Heidegger is a "grounding in the buried essence," a grounding that receives "its direction from out of the autochthonic nearness to the origin." The "illusion of liberation," however, is a "leading away into the rootless foreign," which can "provide no order [*Fug*]."[15] The "deracination of the peoples" as their "self-alienation" is this delivery into the "rootless foreign." The price that they pay for this self-alienation is an illusory freedom.

Consequently, Heidegger proposes a pair of foreigns. To lend the distinction between the two some initial philosophical persuasive force, we must distinguish the ontologically foreign from the ontically foreign. There would be, on the one hand, being itself as the foreign itself and, on the other hand, foreign beings that, among other things, could also appear as ethnic foreigners. Nevertheless, the persuasive force of this distinction should not be overestimated, for Heidegger ascribes the foreign as being itself to both the Greeks and the Germans, and this in a twofold manner.

First, it is the "origin" plain and simple that imparts "rootedness," although—or perhaps precisely *because*—according to Heidegger it is the "assault of the fullness of the ever-strange." "Origin," however, is proper to the Greeks and Germans only in so far as they decide about the "first" and "other beginning." This once again is essential for the second manner of being's foreignness (*Seinsfremdheit*). For there is an exceptional foreign for the Germans: that of the Greeks. This foreign is interpreted by Heidegger in his Hölderlin lecture courses.[16] It belongs in the narrative of the encounter of the Greeks and the Germans, an encounter in which they each "learn their own" through their respective penetration of the other, of what is respectively foreign. Through its establishment in the narrative, the foreign attains the signature of the "beginning" and is thus transformed into one's own (*das Eigene*).

The question, however, is how a signature could be proper to being itself, to this wholly other to beings, a signature that precisely permits the Germans (and the Greeks) "to prepare a site" for it? One can certainly claim that the thinking of being itself bears a Greek provenance. Nevertheless, there is no cause for assuming that being itself would harbor such a provenance, especially since it displays nothing—not even a language—that would make possible its "rootedness" in a particular historical constellation of two peoples.

Here we are in no way denying that philosophy, and along with it the thinking of being, has a history. Nor that the German reception of the "Grecian" since Winckelmann and his writings constitutes a European peculiarity. Without this, the cultural-political project of Goethe or Wagner (two names against which Heidegger long stood hostilely opposed) could not be understood. And so, with his narrative of the being-historical importance of the relationship between the Germans and the Greeks, Heidegger likewise belongs in such a series of great thinkers, poets, and composers. But this does not change the fact that the very idea of being (*Seins*) forbids both the ascription of historical (or historiological) attributes to it and the reservation of a specific narrative for it.[17]

For it is true that being itself, on account of its own self-negativity, is "ever-strange." In being (*Sein*) itself there is nothing that could be known by us after the manner of a being (*ein Seiendes*). Accordingly, the addressee of this "ever-strange" cannot be exclusively a German, a French, a Russian, or a Chinese person. Its addressee is possibly anyone. And the "rootless foreign"? Heidegger determines it continually as "Americanism," more rarely as "Romanism," although even "the French" are incapable of corresponding with the "origin," according to certain statements in the *Black Notebooks*. Regardless, whether Heidegger actually meant something crudely conservative by "Americanism," i.e., that the American is at its core the European principle of nihilistic mass culture, or whether he saw in this the continuation and even the authentic form of "world Judaism"—the one possibility just as much as the other stands for the "rootless foreign."

Doubtless the supposed "hereditary defect of the Germans," this running after the foreign, can be understood only when this foreign takes on a form. For the "peasant" it is already the "city dweller," the one who recommends the "radio apparatus." For the German it may be multiple: one of the figures of the foreign can be "world Judaism" or a "*still* more fundamentally practiced 'Americanism.'" To the extent that "world Judaism," as mentioned above, is "everywhere elusive," it can appear as the "rootless foreign" plain and simple. Heidegger never conceived that precisely in the experience of *this* foreign—if it can even be characterized as "foreign"—one's "own" could have proven itself.

Rather did it become increasingly important for him that the "hereditary defect" exact its consequences. The Germans did not want to be the "people of poets and thinkers." They were not ready to answer the "first beginning" with the "other beginning." This drove Heidegger ever deeper into the thought that even the Germans would have nothing to oppose to global technology. The "rootless foreign" was more powerful, it dominated the Germans, it was always already everywhere. Everything would now be ascribed to "total mobilization" (E. Jünger), more specifically, to "machination." The question remained, which way of life best corresponds to this foreign. After 1945, "homelessness" (*Heimat-losigkeit*) had become "the destiny of the world."[18] Was the triumph of technology not the final victory of "world Judaism"?

After the war, Heidegger remarks in one place that a "foreign essence" surrounds and distorts "our own essence still kept from us."[19] With his customary ambivalence, he further asks "from where" it would all stem, whence "the seduction of the German by a foreign essence, whence this incapacity for politics," "whence the presumption and whence the efficiency with which even what is erroneous and measureless is pursued," "whence the formlessness and lack of essence [*Unwesen*] in everything that accompanies this"? Indeed, the ambivalence lies not in the question, but in the view that there would be a "foreign essence" that seduced "the Germans." The "foreign essence" is a being-historical quantity that can embody itself in factical foreigners. Often for Heidegger, these "foreigners" are simply the Jews.

HEIDEGGER AND HUSSERL

How a philosophical movement conceives itself is firmly tied to the history of its emergence. Generations of philosophers give shape to a conversation on the basis of a common descent. The descent need not be harmonious, it is enough if one can join it from a set range of standpoints. "Phenomenology," as it was able to develop in the twentieth century—particularly in Germany and France and, from there, emanating to the whole of Europe, indeed, to the entire world—received and receives its self-conception from its pair of founding fathers, Edmund Husserl and Martin Heidegger.[1]

This self-conception has established points of reference. Husserl came to Freiburg in 1916. The habilitated Heidegger became his assistant; he "practiced phenomenological seeing, teaching, and learning in Husserl's proximity after 1919," as Heidegger recalls in a position statement from 1963.[2] Heidegger particularly treasures the sixth "Logical Investigation" and speaks of Husserl as the "master."

In addition, in 1926 Heidegger's *Being and Time* was "dedicated to Edmund Husserl in admiration and friendship"—a book that even today still draws those who philosophize under its spell and that even Jürgen Habermas characterized as "the most profound turning-point in German philosophy since Hegel."[3] And even when it became clear that Heidegger's later thinking had basically nothing more to do with Husserl's, one could still point back to the "magnum opus" with its dedication. It all speaks of a time when no one could suspect that German history would painfully inscribe itself even into this founding story of phenomenology.

In the meantime it has become known that Husserl dismissed the book. It is no exaggeration to say he was shocked.[4] He had to recognize that the one whom he had expected to carry on "transcendental phenomenology" had instead struck out on his own path, and in Husserl's eyes an erroneous one. In a letter to Roman Ingarden, Husserl says that he is thinking about writing "an article against Heidegger."[5] In 1934 he speaks of Heidegger's thinking as the "*contemporary* ontology of irrationalism."[6]

It is naturally no small matter that Heidegger dedicated *Being and Time* to Husserl. One can imagine that Heidegger, despite all their differences (not only on technical matters), would have assumed his teacher to be in a position to recognize the towering significance of the work. Psychologically, we must presume Heidegger to have been disappointed, though he never actually acknowledged this. The teacher did not want to learn. And what is a teacher who refuses to learn? Is not a learner the only teacher?

In 1928 Heidegger became Husserl's successor at Freiburg University. The teacher still supported the student for this promotion. The reading of *Being and Time* occurred later. Perhaps a portion of German academic history would look very different today had Husserl read the book immediately upon its release. The difficulty in being able to speak of a *pair* of founding fathers for phenomenology begins with Heidegger's assumption of Husserl's chair.

In the "*Spiegel* Interview" of 1966, Heidegger speaks quite rightly of "our differences of opinion on philosophical matters," which "in the beginning of the thirties" "intensified."[7] Husserl is said to have "settled accounts with Max Scheler and me in public. The clarity of Husserl's statements left nothing to be desired." At Berlin University, Husserl had "spoken before an audience of sixteen hundred." There was report of a "'kind of sport-palace atmosphere.'" The source of this report is known.[8] It is not without significance that after 1945 the Berlin sports palace would come to connote, above all else, Goebbels's call for "total war" in February 1943. Heidegger knew this. Had Husserl publicly agitated against him?

The lecture that Husserl gave at the invitation of the Kant Societies in Frankfurt, Berlin (June 10, 1931), and Halle comes to us with the title "Phenomenology and Anthropology."[9] But what Husserl carries out there he had already presented a year before in greater detail in his "Afterword to *Ideas* I."[10] Notably enough, in this earlier text Heidegger's name does not appear. Husserl speaks of the "situation of German philosophy, in which life-philosophy struggles for predominance, with its new anthropology and its philosophy of 'existence.'"[11] Yet one of the proponents of "existence-philosophy" as characterized there was Heidegger. It was clear who was intended.

The confrontation is measured in tenor, though indeed here and there quite gruff. Husserl defends himself against "reproaches of 'intellectualism' and 'rationalism'" that, in fact, were made by the representatives of those currents either in writing or orally.[12] Nevertheless, in the "objections raised from these sides" Husserl could "recognize nothing justifiable."[13] On the contrary, he assertively emphasized "that one thereby remains stuck in anthropology, whether empirical or a priori."

It is true that Heidegger also publicly criticized Husserl (and did so earlier in private correspondence). But these criticisms cannot be said to have abandoned the level of a purely philosophical dispute. Heidegger's disappointment over the refused recognition of this father figure surely reached deep.[14] Now

Husserl also turned away in the public sphere. Heidegger's presentation of the events in the "*Spiegel* Interview" nevertheless remains unreasonable.

In *Anmerkungen* V, a *Black Notebook* from the end of the 1940s, Heidegger anticipates the self-defense that appears in the "*Spiegel* Interview." Of the Husserl lecture just mentioned, one could speak "sooner of a rally."[15] Husserl is said to have denounced Heidegger's thinking as "unphilosophy," and here Heidegger is able to point to the "Afterword to *Ideas* I." He, however, has "gone past" Husserl.[16] Even as rector he "never undertook the slightest thing against Husserl." It is a lie that Heidegger would have "driven him out of the university and prohibited him entry to the library." Moreover, "his work was never even removed from the seminar library, as was mandatory for Jewish authors."

Once again Heidegger emphasizes that it was a "painful necessity" to "go past" Husserl. Whoever speaks of a "detestable betrayal" knows not that he speaks "only of revenge" and knows "nothing of what happened earlier," namely, "that my own path of thinking was interpreted as a defection, and that recourse was taken to propaganda, as my path was otherwise not to be stopped." The first holds true, the second does not.[17]

Being and Time remains "the worthiest testament" for "what I owe to Husserl—that I learned from him and vouched for his path by not remaining his follower, or ever becoming one."[18] Precisely this, however, "struck against the house rules, long before the talk was of National Socialism and the persecution of Jews."[19] It is more than significant that, for Heidegger, the decisive break lies in Husserl's incapacity to grant the student his own philosophical independence. This break took place before "National Socialism and the persecution of the Jews" was spoken of . . .

With this we abandon the region of difficulties found within a philosophical teacher-student relationship. The potential prob-

lems in the relationship between Heidegger and Husserl go beyond the question of teachers and pupils. By the end of the
1920s, the relationship had been destroyed by forces explicable
neither by philosophical competition, nor by psychological moti-
vations. Heidegger is said to have increasingly made clear that
he was an anti-Semite. Nevertheless, we must not trace his relation to Husserl back to a solely private anti-Semitic *ressentiment*, leaving the philosophical confrontation out of it.[20] Much
more is it a matter of asking whether Heidegger's philosophical
rejection of Husserlian phenomenology was contaminated by a
being-historical anti-Semitism.

In the *Überlegungen* XII from the year 1939 (Husserl died a
year before), Heidegger speaks of an "empty rationality and calculative capacity" of "Judaism."[21] It would be in keeping with this
intellectual casting of Jews that "the more originary and inceptual the future decisions and questions" become, "the more inaccessible" they remain "for this 'race.'" "Thus" Husserl's thinking
can never reach "the region of essential decisions." Heidegger's
"attack," however, is not directed against Husserl "alone" and is
"on the whole inessential"; the attack would go "against the dere-
liction of the question of being, i.e., against the essence of metaphysics as such."

Husserl's thinking stands outside "essential decisions" because it remains caught in abstractions and calculations of the
intellectual kind, as befits "this 'race'" of Jews. To be sure, this
is itself an abstract determination that Heidegger would have to
substantiate through a concrete criticism of Husserl's incapacity
for being-historical decisions. So we have to ask, does he else-
where ever deliver such a critique? Naturally, the presumption
of a being-historically cast "calculative capacity" in the way of
thinking of the Jewish race would render the critique nonsensical from the outset.

In the mentioned *Bemerkungen* V (from the end of the 1940s),

Heidegger sketches a philosophical critique of Husserl. Thus he asks whether "the one who in thinking utters the principle 'to the things [*Sachen*] themselves'" has "already proven himself the expert [*Sachkundige*]."[22] The question is answered in the negative, since "in the matter of thinking" he could "still slip up terribly and with such oversights act against his own principle," and be left "incapable of even sacrificing the principle for the sake of the thing [*Sache*]." "'That which shows itself (what?) from itself'"—Heidegger's approach to phenomenology—is "not only a different formulation of the principle of description that befits the matter [*sachgemäßen Beschreibung*]." Here one "already" sees "the turn of thinking to Ἀλήθεια as an essential trait of being itself." And Heidegger concludes: "Not only does Husserl know nothing of all this, he barricades himself against it."

Certainly, this remark is found in a context where there is no talk of Judaism. It can be understood as a purely philosophical criticism. But while this critique does address Husserl's inability and unwillingness to think in a being-historical manner, Heidegger's earlier remark concerning the "empty rationality and calculative capacity" of Judaism cannot be ignored. It imposes itself on the interpretation all the more.

Moreover, the actual dimension of the criticism is not clear. Already in *Being and Time*, Heidegger indeed speaks of ἀλήθεια, but in no way of Ἀλήθεια.[23] By reading *Being and Time* was Husserl supposed to have obtained the possibility "of thinking the experience of Ἀλήθεια from the experience of the forgetfulness of being"? Without a doubt, no. But Heidegger's criticism is also not posed in such a philological manner. Husserl's thinking as such remains outside the "experience of Ἀλήθεια." It remains bound to metaphysics, without access to the being-historical "turn of thinking to Ἀλήθεια as essential trait of being itself." Husserl did not understand the "future decisions" because the history of being escaped him.

In the "Report on the Results of the Proceedings of the Settlement Committee from December 11 and 13, 1945" of the University of Freiburg [i.e., the University Denazification Committee], where it is a matter, at war's end, of Heidegger's forced retirement, we find a section devoted to Heidegger's "behavior toward Jews."[24] The question as to whether Husserl's "Jewish descent" had played a role in the "discord between Heidegger and his teacher Husserl" is rebutted by the remarks of Heidegger already mentioned. There had been "many more philosophical differences of opinion" that in "1930 or 1931" were also aired in public by Husserl. The report continues: "According to Herr Eucken's knowledge, Husserl was of the mind that Heidegger had turned away from him due to his anti-Semitism. Herr Eucken gave no further statement as to the details of this, as that would not be in accord with Husserl's wishes."[25] Admittedly, Husserl had been dead for seven years. In 1945, remaining "in accord with Husserl's wishes" was perhaps no longer so important. And one can surely ask whether Husserl had privately characterized Heidegger's philosophical critique of him as anti-Semitically motivated.

Husserl did express himself on Heidegger's anti-Semitism, not to Eucken, but to his old student Dietrich Mahnke in a letter from May 1933. Here Husserl describes his disappointing experiences from 1933 in general and with his former student in particular. He speaks sarcastically of the "most beautiful conclusion to this supposedly philosophical intellectual friendship." This he discerns as much in Heidegger's "entirely theatrical" and "publicly performed entrance into the National Socialist party" as also, "in recent years," in "an anti-Semitism coming ever stronger to expression—against even his group of enthusiastic Jewish students as well as among the faculty."[26] So it is possible, even probable, that Husserl had spoken with Eucken in this manner about Heidegger, too.

Now it has long been known that already in a letter from 1916, Heidegger spoke of a "Jewification of our culture and universities," a judgment that many made—even Jews themselves.[27] In retrospect, however, we must now ask whether Heidegger's later being-historical anti-Semitism does not cast new light upon this possibly pure and private *ressentiment*. Was it not Heidegger himself who later repeatedly emphasized—even if erroneously— the being-historical motivation behind his university politics?

In this context, an episode in that Freiburg University administrative "Report" takes on a new significance: Heidegger is said to have asserted that "he had come to a Jew-free faculty and had no wish for a Jew to be appointed."[28] It appears that Heidegger already at the time of his rectorate had pursued a being-historical anti-Semitism. And it is not improbable that he even sacrificed his relation to Husserl to it.

Husserl's remark that he had been reproached with "'intellectualism' and 'rationalism,'" his sketch of Heidegger's thinking as the "contemporary ontology of irrationalism," now appear otherwise when viewed against the background of Heidegger's being-historical anti-Semitism. Certainly, judging anti-Semitic ideas to be "irrational" requires no prior philosophical transformation of these ideas into being-historical relations. But in a consideration of the relation between Heidegger and Husserl it is not unimportant that Heidegger's philosophical aversion to Husserl's phenomenology quite possibly contains anti-Semitic moments from the outset.

The question remains, who spoke of the "persecution of the Jews" and when? Heidegger, in any event, never spoke of this. Now, in recalling his break with Husserl, this word suddenly appears. Why does Heidegger emphasize that the break would have taken place long before the "talk" of "National Socialism and the persecution of the Jews"? Is Heidegger thinking of the time after the war, when one could speak freely about the "persecution of the Jews," without this freedom ever being used for that? Or is Heidegger thinking of the 1930s, of the anti-Semitic propaganda? Was it in this that there was "talk of the persecution of the Jews"? Or is Heidegger thinking of clandestine conversations, of encounters, in which people expressed their revulsion at the rumors of the camps? Could this all be connected with Husserl? When did Heidegger know of the "persecution of the Jews"?

WORK AND LIFE

Heidegger scholarship is often ruled by the maxim that the thought and life of a philosopher are to be distinctly separated. Thus as Walter Biemel stated in his influential Heidegger monograph from 1973: "It is not his life from which we can learn something about his work; his work is his life."[1] Gaining access to his life thus means "following his creative activity, trying to grasp the leading idea behind this activity." Biemel proclaims a unity of work and life in which the work is at the center, around which the life unfolds.

Attributing such importance to the relationship between life and work is justified. In regard to Heidegger's work and life, it is also by and large correct: for Heidegger the work, the literary remains (*Nachlaß*), was ever the radiant center. Indeed, Biemel seems to conclude from this that the life, the telling of this life, the biography, would be meaningless. But this is not in keeping with the thought that the life develops around a center, around a work; for then a trace of the work must be locatable in that life.

"The starting point of philosophy: factical life as *fact*," Heidegger says in an early sketch.[2] This sounds like something different. In this regard factical life—which is each time my "*self-world*," the "personal rhythm" of my life—appears to be a condition of thinking.[3] That would be too rigid. For this reason, Heidegger says at another place that philosophy indeed arises "from factical life experience," but then it "returns back into factical life experience."[4] Philosophy and life—a rhythmic symbiosis.

Philosophy is accordingly no science, for the latter is not only distant from factical life but must necessarily distance itself from it. The scientific judgment can appeal solely to what shows itself in the scientific object. The life of the scientist stands in no relation to this object—at least to the extent that the object typically does not prove to be a phenomenon of factical life (like elementary particles, for example). The life of the philosopher, on the contrary, is intertwined with its object or nonobject.

Thus it is in keeping with Heidegger's life and thought that we regard life "at the hut" as a philosophical act, that we connect his political engagement with his thinking, and that we likewise understand his need to experience "the beat of that god's [Eros's] wings"—something conceded by his wife—all in the context of the work.[5] It is he, the thinker, who demanded from life all that life gave him. What does this have to do, then, with the guiding idea of these considerations, "Heidegger's being-historical anti-Semitism"? Was Heidegger actually an anti-Semite?

Heidegger maintained friendly and courteous dealings with Jews, indeed, even intimate dealings. How could that have been otherwise? Husserl was his teacher, from whom he increasingly distanced himself for philosophical reasons; as rector, Heidegger first supported Jonas Cohn, a Jewish colleague, but then shifted him into retirement under the auspices of the "Law for the Restoration of the Professional Service" in July 1933;[6] he had high regard for his assistant Werner Brock, whom he helped secure a stipendium from Cambridge University in 1933, but thought that he could "not work in seminar," since "the Jews" lack something;[7] not to mention Hannah Arendt, but also Elisabeth Blochmann, with whom he remained in contact until his death; Mascha Kaléko he met at the end of the 1950s and appeared immediately to revere her;[8] Paul Celan, whose poetry he particularly cherished, etc. All these Jewish men and women obviously encountered Heidegger in various ways, and none of these relationships was broken off for anti-Semitic reasons. On the contrary, many even survived the Shoah or were—painfully, as in the case of Celan—begun after it.

If the interpretation in the previous pages is correct, from these and other facts it follows only that, on the one hand, Heidegger as a philosopher formulated anti-Semitic thoughts, while, on the other hand, he lived at times in great accord with Jews. This tension corresponds to a well-known observation in anti-Semitic research.

Hannah Arendt speaks in *The Origins of Totalitarianism* of the "exception Jews."[9] Western European "society" would never have opened the doors of its salons to Jews "in general," but only to these exceptions. Thus these "exception Jews" were caught in an "ambiguity." It was required of them that they be "Jews and yet not *like* Jews."[10] They should thus in no way be like "'mere mortals,'" but rather, like Disraeli, display "exoticism, strangeness, mysteriousness."[11]

According to Arendt this remained the case during the time of the National Socialist persecution. Thus at one place in her book on Eichmann, she writes pointedly: "Hitler himself is said to have known three hundred and forty 'first-rate Jews,' whom he had either altogether assimilated to the status of Germans or granted the privileges of half-Jews."[12] Here she still believes that Reinhard Heydrich, the organizer of the Shoah, himself would have been a "half-Jew." That has turned out to be false, though Heydrich had to concern himself with this rumor throughout his life. Other famed examples of "exceptional Jews" could be named, such as the episode from Richard Wagner's biography in which he insisted that the debut performance in Bayreuth of his "festival play for the consecration of the stage," *Parsifal,* be conducted by Hermann Levi.

However such relations have appeared individually—to have an anti-Semitic attitude and to traffic with Jews amicably and caringly were not and are not mutually exclusive. On the contrary, the exception appears to confirm the rule. Would that also apply to Heidegger? Regardless, with him one also finds two formulations that seem to allow us to conclude that he did make exceptions in regard to Jews. One concerns his relation to Arendt, which I will go into in a subsequent chapter. The other concerns Gotthold Ephraim Lessing, whom he once ostentatiously named a "*German* thinker"—and precisely in so doing thereby indirectly marked him as not German.[13]

Finally, it holds particularly for being-historical anti-Semitism that it represents only with great difficulty that which it is directed against, that which would be embodied in particular persons. For what it represents does not show itself, but hides itself. How could it be seen if it were to appear? Every possible "image" goes right past being-historical anti-Semitism and never corresponds to it. But is there an anti-Semitism without a concrete "image" of the vilified Jew? With Heidegger this appears to be the case.

It might follow from this that Heidegger never needed to make "exceptions" in his concrete dealings with Jews. It was already clear to him that "world Judaism" had no face. To be sure, there were the "emigrants let out." But as Heidegger formulated it, their role was merely to incite "world Judaism." This, however, remained "everywhere elusive," i.e., invisible. We might also find here a reason why Heidegger reserved these anti-Semitic passages for the *Black Notebooks.* Ultimately, being-historical anti-

Semitism and the prevailing anti-Semitic conceptions grounded in race theory—conceptions Heidegger rejected without repudiating the concept of race—cannot be brought into accord.

The work is the center of the life. All ways of life radiate out from it and lead back to it. This remains the case even in the *Black Notebooks*. Between the written expressions about the Jews and his life with them Heidegger apparently sensed no grave contradiction. "World Judaism" was precisely "everywhere elusive." Indeed, as with everything that a philosopher thinks, his work is put into a still more intensive light when that life, determined by the work, is also taken into account. Supporting this is Heidegger's reunion with Hannah Arendt after the Shoah.

ANNIHILATION AND
SELF-ANNIHILATION

In the *Black Notebooks*, the narrative topography of the history of being is demarcated by terms and concepts that depict the Second World War so as to revise it in a being-historical manner. Alongside the "Germans"—those representatives of the "other beginning"—Heidegger places the "Russians." As the "Germans" can be being-historically distinguished from "National Socialism," so too the "Russians" from "Bolshevism." Then there appears, with growing importance, the being-historical power of "Americanism," the heir to "England." "France" also surfaces, the nation of Descartes, the nation of Paris, a nation that began to increasingly interest Heidegger at the end of the 1940s. "Christianity" is marked as an obstacle for the "beginning." Even the "Asiatic" is named, neutrally alongside the "Chinese" (*Chinesentum*), a previously employed defamation that sees in China only a land of massive exploitation. And also, to be sure, "Judaism" and "world Judaism," or even "Jewry" (*Judenschaft*).

This topography is brought into a specific order, not to say a determinate battle formation (τάξις): on the one side, the agents of "machination"—England, Americanism, Bolshevism, i.e., being-historically understood "Communism," and "Judaism" (also "Christianity"); on the other, the sites of "beginning"— "Greece," "Germany," and "Russia."

It is doubly determined. On the one hand, we can recognize in this the lines of the front in the war. In the *Überlegungen*, written between 1938 and 1941, Heidegger attentively follows the events of the war. He is interested in the "'historiological' incidents."[1] On the other hand, the topography proves to be a staging of the drama of the history of being. The lines of the front are written into a narrative in which "beginning" and "end" form the two essential formal elements. The beginning is ascribed to German "thinking and poetizing" (always in reference to the pre-Socratic "Greeks"), the "end" to the forces of machination. The double determination of this topography thus follows Heidegger's heavily emphasized distinction between historiology (*Historie*) and the history of being (*Seinsgeschichte*).

The double determination of the war constantly oscillates between a historiological and a being-historical significance, and not only in the *Überlegungen*, but also in the *Anmerkungen* begun in 1942. On the historiological level, the relation between beginning and end is a matter of "decisions," of a "destruction," indeed of a "devastation whose dominance can no longer be touched by the catastrophes of war or catastrophic wars," though it "can be attested" by such.[2] The historiological war is thus "testament" to the history of being. In itself, however, it no longer concerns who is militarily victorious or defeated. The war attests much more to a "decision" in which "everything" becomes "slaves to the history of beyng."[3] A slave, however, is not only someone who is compelled to work, but rather someone who through his work is of service. How then do these "slaves"—for example, the Jews—serve the history of beyng?

The being-historical significance of the war consists in the "purification *of being* from its deepest deformation by the precedence of beings."[4] This is for Heidegger the *"highest completion of technology."* The completion of this highest stage of technology would be "achieved when technology, as consuming, has nothing more to consume—other than itself."⁵ He then asks: "In what form is this self-annihilation implemented?" The purification of being is a "self-annihilation" of technology that takes place in war. Like Heraclitus, Heidegger too thinks of a world conflagration, one that would liberate the world from the "precedence of beings."⁶ History empties into an *apocalyptic reduction*. Is there still a beginning, or is there now only an end?

The apocalyptic reduction of history is a further narrative that is built into the already prevailing narratival topography of the history of being. Heidegger probably first thought of the self-annihilation of machination at the moment when the war took on a "total" character. And now the topography must be populated with protagonists. The front is inscribed into a self-annihilation. World Judaism assumes its role, as do Americanism and National Socialism.

This role is ambiguous. To understand the ambiguity we must distinguish among figures of the end within this decision between beginning and end: "destruction," "devastation," "annihilation," "self-annihilation." The apocalyptic-reductive role of world Judaism is an essential factor in differentiating between "annihilation," "destruction," and "self-annihilation." Indeed, Judaism is perhaps nothing other than the apocalyptic reduction itself.

Heidegger speaks of "annihilation" in the exoteric text of the lecture course *On the Essence of Truth* from the winter semester of 1933/34. He interprets the famed fragment 53 of Heraclitus, where πόλεμος is said to be the father and king of all things, making some into gods, others into humans, some into slaves, others into the free. This dictum is frequently interpreted by Heidegger at this time.

The πόλεμος is understood as a "standing against the enemy."⁷ The enemy would be "each and every person who poses an essential threat to the Dasein of the people and its individual members." The enemy in no way needs to be "external," i.e., he need not show himself in the form of an enemy nation. Rather it could "seem as if there were no enemy." Then it would be a "fundamental requirement to find the enemy, to expose the enemy to the light, or even first to make the enemy." Accordingly, it is irrelevant whether the enemy actually exists or not. Dasein needs an enemy.

The enemy "can have attached itself to the innermost roots of the Dasein of a people and can set itself against this people's own essence and act against it." The enemy is thus an enemy of the "essence." Thus the "struggle" becomes "all the fiercer and harder and tougher." For "it is often far more difficult and wearisome to catch sight of the enemy as such, to bring the enemy into the open" and "to prepare the attack looking far ahead with the goal of total annihilation."[8]

The enemy of "essence" is thus met with "total annihilation." This discourse, which has nothing to do with Heraclitus's dictum, is obviously brutal. Possibly, Heidegger wants to oppose the new authorities. For the semantics of the formulation are contemporary. Is it not a "parasite" that would have attached itself to the "innermost roots of the Dasein of a people"? Is it necessary to characterize the "enemy" any further?

Heidegger keeps silent. But in a later passage he says: "Marxism cannot be defeated once and for all unless we first confront the doctrine of ideas and its two-millennia-long history."[9] It is "Marxism" that is considered the enemy of essence. In the consciousness of the 1930s, Marx is the "Jew Marx."[10] Unmistakably, Marxism appears as a figure of metaphysics, that is, of the history of being. Plato's "doctrine of Ideas" is presented as the presupposition of Marxism.

Unstated here is that Marxism, i.e., Judaism, becomes subject to "total annihilation." The enemy of essence, however, must itself be active. It must attack. The πόλεμος, as Heidegger construes it, demands this. At the time of the war, then, Heidegger

ANNIHILATION AND SELF-ANNIHILATION // 73

altered his narrative of the history of being. The historiological events required a constant revision of being-historical thinking. The Jews are now not simply the enemy of the essence of the "Dasein of a people," but rather take on a "polemical" role in the "Christian West" itself:

> In the period of the Christian West, i.e., of metaphysics, Jewry is the principle of destruction. [It is what is] destructive in the overturning of the completion of metaphysics—i.e., of Hegel's metaphysics by Marx. Spirit and culture become the superstructure of "life"—i.e., of the economy, i.e., of the organization—i.e., of the biological—i.e., of the "people."[11]

"Jewry" destroys the metaphysical structure of the "Christian West," insofar as this structure completes itself in Hegel's philosophy. Marx, who claimed to have stood Hegel upon his head, lays the tracks that lead directly into machination and, now, the Third Reich. The sequence "superstructure of 'life'—i.e., of the economy, i.e., of the organization—i.e., of the biological—i.e., of the 'people'" gets to the heart of it: Marx, the destructive Jew, is the precursor to National Socialism.

(Hitler, whose anti-Semitism is brutally biological, speaks in *Mein Kampf* of the "destructive principle of the Jew"—to be sure, in relation to Theodor Mommsen's notorious formulation of the Jew as the "effective ferment of cosmopolitanism and national decomposition."[12] And "the Jew" is for Hitler without further ado always also "the Marxist.")

The "principle of destruction" is the same as the "world-historical task" of "uprooting beings from being" that Heidegger ascribed to "world Judaism" around 1940.[13] "Jewry" "destroys" the order of difference between beings and being. Marx, who occupied himself in his dissertation with Democritus and Epicurus, is identified as a Jew by the materialist foundation of his thinking.[14]

EXCURSUS

Emmanuel Levinas attempted in his essay "Heidegger, Gagarin, and Us," published in 1961, to lay out the most important difference between Judaism, Heidegger, and—they are explicitly named—the Heideggerians. In all essentials, this concerns the topographic order of the world emphasized by Heidegger and the destruction of this order by the technology affirmed by Judaism.

"One's implementation in a landscape, one's attachment to *Place*," this would be the "splitting of humanity into natives and strangers." In this perspective, "technology is less dangerous than any spirit of a place." It attacks "the privileges of this enrootedness and the related sense of exile." Technology "wrenches us out of the Heideggerian world and the superstitions surrounding *place*."[15]

Against this, Gagarin showed us how we could abandon place. Thus Levinas says: "For one hour, man existed beyond any horizon—everything around him was sky, or, more exactly, everything was geometrical space. A man existed in the absolute of homogeneous space."[16] In the year 1961, Yuri Gagarin orbited the earth for 106 minutes in the space capsule *Vostok I*.

Decisive, however, is that Levinas relates the idea of replacing "place" with "homogeneous space" to Judaism. Judaism "has not sublimated idols—on the contrary, it has demanded that they be destroyed." "Like technology," Judaism "has demystified the universe." Through its "abstract universalism" it damages "imaginations and passions." Indeed, it has "discovered man in the nudity of his face."[17]

Even Levinas speaks of a *destruction*. In Heidegger's eyes it concerns the "destruction" proceeding from universalism, the destruction of machination, which is still no "annihilation." It is a little uncanny to see to what extent Levinas affirms the apocalyptic reduction of the history of being. It is he who, coming from the other side, writes the confrontation between "universalist" Judaism and Heidegger into the apocalyptic reduction.

Heidegger assigns all this to the history of metaphysics. Sometime at the start of the 1940s he noted the following about Platonism:

> The estimation of the ἀγαθόν [the good] as the τελευταία ἰδέα [last Idea] *beyond* ἀλήθεια [truth] and the ἀληθές [true] as γιγνωσκόμενον [what is known] is the first, i.e., the authentic, step that goes the furthest toward the serial production of long-range bomber planes and the invention of radio-technological news reports, with whose help the former are deployed in service of the unconditioned mechanization of the globe and humanity, equally predetermined by that step.[18]

Heidegger turns his interpretation of metaphysics upon contemporary and pressing phenomena. "Long-range bomber planes" destroy and annihilate cities.

Plato's doctrine of Ideas, which is bound up with the denigration of ἀλήθεια in Heidegger's eyes, is the cause of that "serial production." Everything that is produced requires a model. This model, this paradigm, is delivered by Plato in the Ideas. This is also the argument for why Heidegger conceives of Marxism as a kind of Platonism. For him, Platonism is a philosophy of "production."

But what are here serially produced are as much long-range bomber planes as radio-technological news reports. Heidegger rightly conceives that the airplanes presuppose the radio. Also Platonism takes the step that "goes the furthest"—in the sense of technology—insofar as it carries the long-distance bomber planes far off into enemy territory.

Is it a coincidence that Levinas speaks of Gagarin's capsule *Vostok I* and Heidegger of "long-range bomber planes"? According to Heidegger, both serve destruction, both have abandoned the earth and move about in universal space. This portends that for Heidegger the Platonic Idea and Judaism are connected. Augustine, in any event, asks himself in book 8 of *The City of God* whether Plato could have known the prophets, and first among them Jeremiah.[19] He comes to a negative judgment, but nevertheless says that he would *almost* like to agree with the claim that Plato must have known those books. Judaism, Platonism, Christianity—three figures of the universal that Heidegger attacks in the *Black Notebooks*.

///////////////////////

The history of being arrives at the completed apocalyptic reduction there where the "enemy" no longer exists, the enemy who, in whatever way, threatens the "Dasein of the people." History itself must make the decision. Now annihilation becomes self-annihilation. But self-annihilation can now, according to Heidegger, affect each and every thing. Machination is total, makes no exceptions. At one point Heidegger speaks of the self-annihilation of communism, i.e., of being-historical communism as he construes it, according to which there is no difference between Bolshevism and Americanism in regard to their supposed promise of universal mediocrity. Then he speaks, after the war, of the self-annihilation of the Germans and—still before the end of the war—of the self-annihilation of the "Jewish." He says:

> Only when what is essentially "Jewish" in the metaphysical sense battles against the Jewish is the pinnacle of self-annihilation in history achieved; assuming that what is "Jewish" has everywhere monopolized dominance entirely for itself, such that even the battle against "the Jewish," and this first of all, becomes servitude to this.[20]

Self-annihilation does not need to be understood everywhere as *physical* annihilation. Rather, there is according to Heidegger even a "self-annihilation of humanity," in which the modern sub-ject as "last man" (Nietzsche) transitions into its "ending."²¹ On the other hand, however, there is also a self-annihilation of the "opponent." For this, "'politics'" in its "modern essence" would have to do nothing more than "trick the opponent into a situa-tion" in which the only option is "self-annihilation."²² Presum-ably, in this passage Heidegger thinks of Americanism; indeed, he says in the same place: "One discovers first and late enough and even then only in half-measures, 'Americanism' as a politi-cal rivalry."

But that the oscillation of the concept of self-annihilation would have as a consequence an indifferent significance cannot be justified. Much more must every single nuance of meaning be observed. For this, we must take notice of *when* Heidegger speaks about, for example, the self-annihilation of the "'Jewish'" and the self-annihilation of the German. At this point, the testimo-nial character of the *Black Notebooks* is relevant. As in the lecture courses, it is important to observe when Heidegger carried out what changes to his narrative of the history of being.

The apocalyptic reduction proves to be the self-annihilation of technology. The narrative topography of Heidegger's thinking displays a being-historical unity of "Americanism," "England," "Bolshevism," "Communism," "National Socialism," and "Juda-ism," more specifically, "world Judaism." All of these protago-nists of the history of being are determined by a "marked gift for calculation," a gift, admittedly, that Heidegger explicitly ascribes to the Jews. They move about in a worldless space in long-range bomber planes and space capsules. They are perhaps the (in-)authentic agents of machination.

Before the war's end, before the "end," these agents of machi-nation are affected by self-annihilation. What is at stake is the other beginning. The decision requires that this beginning must occur without victors or losers. For the distinction between victors and losers immediately relapses into technology. Technology must annihilate itself, while dragging its agents along with it.

But the end of the war shows that the agents of machination have persevered. Now they drive the Germans into self-annihilation. Heidegger speaks of a "death machinery" that has transformed "the German people and land into a single *Kz* [*Konzentrationslager*, concentration camp]."[23] The self-annihilation of machination remains outstanding, which can only have the self-annihilation of the Germans as its consequence.

The question remains, how are we to understand the self-annihilation of the "'Jewish'" and of the "Jewish" (do quotation marks in Heidegger always have a darker, more sinister meaning?). The "'Jewish'" is now apparently machination. In this sense, the National Socialists, and with them the Americans, English, and Bolsheviks, are all representatives of what is "'Jewish.'"[24] Whatever opposes this falls into its "servitude," thinks according to its rules. The "Jewish," however, is—what else could it be?—the character of factical Jews. The self-annihilation of machination occurs in the form of the annihilation of the "Jewish" by the "'Jewish'": Auschwitz—the "self-annihilation" of Judaism? The thought annihilates the annihilated once again.

AFTER THE SHOAH

There is no known public expression of Heidegger's in which he takes a position in regard to the Shoah. Two allusions in the *Bremen Lectures*, in which Heidegger speaks of a "production of corpses in the gas chambers and extermination camps" (as Hannah Arendt also does around the same time), do not count as expressions about the Shoah.[1] Such an expression would not have to be an "apology," but perhaps an attempt to let thinking founder against what occurred, or perhaps, in an act of courage, to mourn.

In the meantime, we know generally how difficult it was to speak in such a way about the Shoah. In Germany, a broad, public discussion of it was basically first initiated by the four-part, thoroughly problematic American television miniseries *Holocaust* in 1978. To be sure, poets and thinkers had already written about it: Hannah Arendt at any rate, Theodor W. Adorno, and likewise Paul Celan in the "Death Fugue." Even Ernst Jünger in "The Peace"—this plea from the end of the Second World War—speaks of the "dens of murder" that "will haunt man's memory to the end of time." They would be the "true monuments of this war."[2] To be sure, the conversation and the sober recognition of what occurred were without doubt painful—and thus difficult.

Of particular importance for Heidegger was the reunion with Hannah Arendt, his highly gifted former student, his lover. He communicated to her in a letter from the beginning of 1933 that "in university issues," he was "just as much an anti-Semite" as he was "ten years ago in Marburg, where, because of this anti-Semitism, I even earned Jacobsthal's and Friedländer's support," an ambivalent remark, since he then adds: "And above all it cannot touch my relationship to you."[3] Heidegger formulates the "exception." Indeed Arendt never even hinted that she might have felt herself to be an "exceptional Jew" in her relations with him. Apart from his academic reservation against Jews, Heidegger had comported himself toward them as toward any others.[4]

But the expression shows that Heidegger could voice an anti-Semitism to Arendt of the sort not uncommon in the 1920s and 1930s. His was directed against the Jews in the universities above all. In this regard he speaks in a letter from October 18, 1916, of the "Jewification [Verjudung] of our culture and universities"—a situational assessment that at this time, as I have already mentioned, was so common as to be even shared by Jews.[5] Even Arendt herself seems not to have objected completely to Heidegger's anti-Semitism "in university issues" before 1933, before the introduction of the "Laws of Coordination" (Gleichschaltungsgesetzes). Indeed, she regarded Heidegger as a universal cultural phenomenon. Heidegger had not yet arrived at being-historical anti-Semitism, something with which she most likely never became familiar.

It was also Arendt who, in a letter from Elfride Heidegger in April 1969, was asked to investigate the sale price for the manuscript of Being and Time. As an explanation for the request, Elfride Heidegger states, "we know nothing of money"—although indeed Fritz Heidegger, her husband's brother, was active for decades in the Volksbank of Meßkirch.[6] Was it an accident that in contemplating the sale of the manuscript, the married couple thought of the Jew Arendt? Did she understand something of money? In the "official" explanations of Heidegger of the past decades, Elfride was held to be the anti-Semite, not her husband. Arendt, in any case, complied with the request without delay.

What Heidegger and Arendt spoke about after their reunion in 1950 is not known. It is unthinkable that Arendt would broach the Shoah. In a letter from April 1950 Heidegger mentions "that the fate of the Jews and the Germans" would "indeed" have "its own truth," for which "our historiological calculation is no match"; an ambivalent remark, since it grants much leeway to interpretation (in any event, the *ja* [indeed] and the *je* [each] in Heidegger's handwriting are barely distinguishable).[7] Even less univocal is Heidegger's statement from a letter a month later, in which he proclaims that there was "another shift in 1937/38" in which "Germany's catastrophe became clear" to him.[8] With the highest probability, all the anti-Semitic remarks in the *Black Notebooks* stem from a later date. It could indeed be the case that Heidegger had reasons for not linking the "catastrophe of Germany" with such remarks. The authentic catastrophe of Germany, being wrecked by "machination," was something different. But was it really something different?

With whom could he otherwise have touched upon the topic of the Shoah? All possible witnesses that are known to me either do not remember having spoken with him about it, or are keeping silent. All known correspondences are equally silent. Just one letter, which Herbert Marcuse sent to Heidegger in August 1947, breaks the silence. Heidegger's evasive answer is well-known.[9]

The *Black Notebooks* break the silence for a moment, the deathly silence (*das Totschweigen*). Provoked by the placards that were distributed by the Psychological Warfare Division of the Supreme Headquarters of the Allied Powers of Europe, Heidegger refers to the Shoah. On the placards with the title "These Disgraceful Deeds: Your Guilt!" there were photographs depicting the liberated concentration camps. Looking back, Heidegger attempts to wrest a meaning here for "destiny."

"We" would be, just as before, "in what is inconspicuously precious of a spared treasure."[10] Indeed for the sake of "*allowing*" ourselves therein, "we would have to first experience what is our own [*das Eigene*] and be freed *to* this [zu *ihm ge-freyt seyn*]; at the same time, however, the foreign would have to allow us, in the sense of an *assistance* [Hilfe], which would presuppose no less than a free-freeing attitude [*freye-freyend-Gesinnung*]." One's "own" must be experienced in order to remain in the "spared treasure." The reference to a "foreign" that would have to "allow" us something is nearly incomprehensible. How have the "foreigners"—and very often the term "foreigners" characterizes Jews—"assisted" us? Have they allowed (ge*lassen*) us or abandoned (ver*lassen*) us? Or are the "foreigners" here indeed the "Greeks," who nevertheless could be so characterized only under the being-historical conditions of Heidegger's Hölderlin interpretations, and to whom certainly no historiological actuality of assistance could be ascribed. The philosopher then also adds: "How dark it is around all of these simple things—and nevertheless—how close is this possibility of a proper destiny—which many are required to carry out."

He continues:

Would, for example, the *misjudgment* of this destiny—which indeed does not belong to us—would the oppression in the world-will [*Weltwollen*]—thought in terms of destiny—not be a still more essential "guilt" and a "collective guilt"—the magnitude of which could not at all—in essence not even once—be measured by the atrocities of the "gas chambers"; a guilt—more uncanny than all publicly "decried" "crimes"—one that certainly in the future no one could ever excuse. Does "one" intimate that already now the German people and country is a single *Kz* [*Konzentrationslager*, concentration camp]—one that "the world" nevertheless still has not "seen" and that "the world" also does not *want* to see—*this* not-wanting is still more willful than our *lack of will* against a *National Socialism* running wild.

The "misjudgment" of this "destiny," i.e., of being allowed to remain in "what is inconspicuously precious of a spared treasure," is characterized as the "world-will." The temporal structure of the context links the past with the present. The "spared treasure" still belongs to us, but "we must" first "experience what is our own." The "world-will," however, is apparently something contemporary (*aktuelles*). It still corresponds to that "destiny" which, precisely because it is "destiny," we do not have at our disposal. Were "we" to be "oppressed" in this "world-will"—now, after the end of the war—then this "oppression" would be a "guilt," "the magnitude of which could not at all—in essence not even once—be measured by the atrocities of the 'gas chambers.'" The "world-will" of the "Germans" is being-historically more important than the "atrocities of the 'gas chambers.'" And why the quotation marks around "gas chambers"?

This "not wanting to see" that "already now the German people and country" is "a single *Kz*" would be "still *more willful* than our *lack of will*" against the degeneracy of National Socialism. Both expressions are directed at the victors, the Allies. Their politics, namely, of restricting the German "world-will," would be more criminal than the mass murder that "certainly in the future no one could ever excuse."

The argumentation is muddled. There is a German "destiny" of the "world-will," an experience of one's "own" with the "assistance" of the "foreign." This "destiny" is elevated against a "*National Socialism* running wild." Accordingly it in no way leads to the "atrocities of the 'gas chambers,'" which are attributed to a degenerate National Socialism. But now the crimes of the Allies could even exceed these "'crimes'" (why the quotation marks?), crimes that Heidegger concedes.

All this confirms the answer to Marcuse, in which it is bemoaned that the "Allies" were able to murder "'East Germans'" before "the world public," "while the bloody terror of the Nazis in point of fact had been kept a secret from the German people."[11] In *Anmerkungen* II, Heidegger speaks of a "*death machinery* set into motion," which should effect the "utter annihilation" of the Germans. And Heidegger adds to this:

> That this machinery would only be the "punishment" for National Socialism, or even only the mere spawn of vengefulness, one may still for some time make a few fools believe. But in truth, one has found the wished-for opportunity—no, over the last 12 years one has *co*-organized that opportunity and done so consciously, so as to set this devastation in motion. If reservations now enter, then they arise only for a calculation that looks to insure that this machinery not disturb its own business dealings too abruptly.

This remark, Heidegger emphasizes, would "no longer be said in public for a reader," but rather would belong "to the destiny of beyng itself and its stillness."[12] How is it said in the *Protocols*? If a non-Jewish state should hazard to proceed against the Jews ("against us"), "then we would have to unleash world war." Was it not the Jews who plunged the Germans into their "catastrophe"? And if this was an erroneous insinuation, Heidegger's view that someone "over the last 12 years" would have "*co*-organized" an "opportunity" to annihilate the Germans is more erroneous still.

Approximately two years later, i.e., around the years 1947 and 1948, Heidegger takes up the same thought once again. He critically assesses the habit of historically emphasizing the dates "1933" and "1945." To do so is "perhaps entirely wrong, to calculate in this way and to take history only historiologically, although the entire modern European world" proceeds "calculatingly in this way with Germany."[13] Indeed, the Germans "still have not yet" noticed "what happens right in front of them and that this calculating has not yet reached the end of calculation." There "still" remains "the task" "*to exterminate the Germans spiritually and historically.*" An "old spirit of revenge" makes its way "upon the earth." The "intellectual history of this revenge" will "never be written," since that would hinder "the revenge itself." It never reaches "a public awareness," for "publicity" itself would already be "this revenge."

The "spirit of revenge" is a spirit of calculation, which is not yet at its end.[14] The "spiritual and historical" extermination of the Germans is still outstanding. Heidegger no longer speaks of a "death machinery"; the forecast for a physical extinction has not been fulfilled. Nevertheless, what did not escape annihilation was Heidegger's narrative of the being-historical special role of the Greeks and the Germans. He probably detected that the time for *this* philosophical story was past. But was it past because a "spirit of revenge" had come over the Germans? Or was the narrative of a special role for the Germans—however this appeared—instead itself annihilated in the annihilation of the Jews?

Although we find no reference to the Shoah in Heidegger's statements in the sources mentioned up to now, he did indeed at one point seize upon words to address this. In a poem composed after their reunion, after the first return—and what a return—to Hannah Arendt, Heidegger writes:

Only to you

THOUGHT AND TENDER

"Thought" —
Oh, help me risk
saying this.

Listen! "Thought"
now means:
unawakening:
horrifyingly transposed
into all the chasms of that wrath,
then plunging away
into the lamentations upon lamentations
of your blood, oh hear it,
and my [relation] to-you
henceforth cast into a "woe! ask!";
the log of this, you
pile upon me with every coming, as the burden
that grips me close, ever closer, ever more deeply,
pulling on the sway of every emotion,
draining away the tenderness of the touch![15]

The poem is in keeping with what Arendt found distinctive in Heidegger. The thinking, the event of thinking, "now" becomes an "unawakening," "transposing." "Now" the thinker has recognized the "wrath" that sounds in the lamentation of the Jewish "blood." "Now" would "my to-you" have become a painful question, "the log of this, you / pile upon me with every coming as the burden." Heidegger here plays upon a verse of Hölderlin's, in whose "Mnemosyne" it says:

And much,
As a load of logs
upon the shoulders, must be
Retained. But evil are
The paths.[16]

It is noteworthy that the "log" is piled up from the coming "as the burden."

In the intimate dedication ("Only to you"), what Heidegger could not say or indeed even feel in any other form now becomes possible. The "burden" becomes palpable in the encounter with the survivor, with the (former) lover, who escaped the crimes. The thinker appears to bear witness to the far-reaching consequences that lie in the reunion—as though the Shoah first became known to him in his nearness to Arendt. What does this poem risk with its admission of a "burden" in thinking? Perhaps everything, perhaps nothing.

Hannah Arendt appears to have reflected upon that. The first note from her *Thought Journals* from June 1950 reads: "The *wrong* that one has done is the burden on the shoulders, something one carries because one has loaded it upon oneself."[17] It then concerns a "gesture of forgiveness," one that would destroy the "equality and thereby the foundation of human relations so radically," that "really, in accordance with such an act, no relation should be possible any longer." For Arendt the return to Germany was a question of "forgiveness," not only toward Heidegger.

Indeed, what did she really think about Heidegger? In a letter to Jaspers from 1946 she characterized him as a "potential murderer," as a teller of "inane lies" with a "clearly pathological streak."[18] In the reunion, this was irrelevant. Other attempts at a distancing, like the characterization of Heidegger as a "fox," remain in view of what happened quite harmless.[19] What would she have said if she had known of Heidegger's anti-Semitic notes? What would all those have said who are named in the very first sentence of this book? Would Karl Löwith have resumed contact? Would Celan have visited Heidegger?

Otherwise asked: how will we deal with Heidegger's being-historical anti-Semitism in relation to the Shoah? It is no longer up for debate whether one should defend (if one can) Heidegger's "political error" against a public whose purported "political correctness" already warps the issue, whether voluntarily or not. There is an anti-Semitism in Heidegger's thinking that—as befits a thinker—undergoes an (impossible) philosophical grounding, but that does not get beyond two or three stereotypes. The being-historical construction makes it all the worse. It is this which could lead to a contamination of this thinking.

One of the last direct utterances about the Jews in the *Black Notebooks* reads:

> "Prophecy" is a technique of defense against the destinal of history [*Geschicklichen der Geschichte*]. It is an instrument of the will to power. That the great prophets are Jews is a fact whose secret has still not been considered. (Note for a jackass: this remark has nothing to do with "anti-Semitism." This is so foolish and so reprehensible, like the bloody—and, above all, the unbloody—actions of Christianity against "the heathens." That even Christianity denounces anti-Semitism as "un-Christian" belongs to the highly cultivated refinement of its power technique.)[20]

To begin with, in this note the façade just crumbles. That is, if the utterance concerning the "death machinery" at work on the Germans was to be said only "to the destiny of beyng itself and its stillness," now it is noted "for a jackass" (i.e., for the public?) that what is said here would have "nothing to do with 'anti-Semitism.'" But what is said? In principle, the following: forecasting and prediction are directed against an understanding of the "destinal of history," which strongly recalls the Greek μοῖρα, the unknowable spinning of the threads of fate, to which even the Greek gods themselves were exposed.

With this Heidegger appears to assume that the prophet primarily speaks about the future, and not critically against the present. Moreover, he ignores that in the stories of being chosen to be a prophet, being seized by God is described often enough as a bitter fate (cf. Ezekiel). The speech of the prophets is continually contested and set upon, and this by other Jews themselves. Accordingly, the "office" of prophet would be thoroughly comparable to that of the self-sacrificing poet that Heidegger had found in Hölderlin alone.[21]

For the thinker, prophetic speech is a "technique," an "instrument of the will to power." Moreover, it hides an unthought "secret." What does he want to signify by this? Through their "'prophecy,'" have the Jews successfully "*co*-organized" "in the last 12 years" the downfall of the Germans? Again we brush up against this pronouncement. Can a philosopher insinuate something like this? Does this not give the impression that the thinker has strayed into occultism, one for which all words fail us? Or must we indeed diagnose an anti-Semitic paranoia?

What Heidegger means in regard to the "secret" of the Jewish prophets he does not take to be anti-Semitism. The rationale for this assuagement is in any case not very convincing. Anti-Semitism is compared to the relationship of Christians to the "'heathens.'" That Christians took action against non-Christians would be just as stupid as anti-Semitism. To condemn anti-Semitism in this Christian way would belong to the "power technique" of the Christians. What is so foolish and so reprehensible in anti-Semitism itself is not at all expressed—rather, Heidegger uses it only as a foil for the sake of denouncing the foolishness and reprehensibility of Christendom. Additionally, he appears to hold "above all, the unbloody actions" to be especially questionable, i.e.. probably the theological condemnation of non-Christians by Christians. Anti-Semitism for Heidegger is not "so foolish and so reprehensible" because it is located within acts of the "will to power." Rather he finds it foolish and reprehensible because, unlike philosophy, it is not able to see through these acts.

As little as Heidegger can disperse the suspicion of anti-Semitism, so much do we have cause to say that he directly founded a further type of it. For him, Judaism and Christianity converge in the technological actuality of the "will to power." For this reason, the truly severe attacks on Christians and Jesuits in the *Black Notebooks* bear a peculiar tone. That there was a Christian anti-Semitism does not contradict this view.

Heidegger's anti-Semitic statements have a direction. The more the "planetary war" approaches its end, the more the formulations shift their emphasis from a characterization of the Jews as agents of machination to Judaism as a religion that, in its connection with Christianity, plays a disastrous role in the history of being. "Jewish-Christian monotheism" is represented as the origin of the "modern system of total dictatorship," a well-known strategy of Heidegger's, according to which National Socialism is an epiphenomenon of Judaism.[22]

Now Heidegger's openness to the "gods," to polytheism, becomes manifest.[23] "Jehovah" would be "that one of the gods who presumes to make himself the chosen God and no longer suffers any other God beside him."[24] The play on "chosen people" is significant. The philosopher asks and answers the following: "What is a god who, against all others, arrogates to himself the status of being chosen? In any event, he is never 'the' god unqualifiedly, assuming that what is meant by this could ever be divine. How could it, when the divinity of god resides in the great calm out of which he recognizes the other gods." Again, Heidegger writes himself into the German *Sonderweg* (special path), which runs from Winckelmann and on past Hölderlin, Schelling, and Nietzsche, leading up to Heidegger himself, upon which it would be possible to long for other gods back before Christianity or out beyond it. The topology of "first" and "other beginning" surfaces:

> From here one can assess what the remembrance of the first beginning in Greece—a beginning that remains outside of Judaism, and that means outside of Christianity—signifies for thinking into the concealed inceptual essence of the history of the West.[25]

The decision is significant: the "Greece" of philosophy is played out against the "Judaism" and "Christianity" of religion. To be sure, the differences between thinking and believing are conspicuous. Even Leo Strauss, a student of Heidegger's, emphasized them—without, however, emphasizing the supposed consequences of those differences that obviously interested Heidegger.[26] The decision for a Greek beginning of Europe need not have any anti-Semitic consequences.

Whether Heidegger's references to "monotheism" make claims that can be transferred into an extant critical-religious discourse is questionable.[27] Certainly one could conceive that "polytheism" would influence political philosophy in specific ways. But this can not be shown in Plato, for example, nor had Heidegger himself thought about this. On the contrary, Heidegger's reservation regarding democracy and his aversion to it are maintained across the entirety of his thinking. Accordingly, we must proceed from the fact that Heidegger's remarks on the religion of Judaism do not overcome his being-historical anti-Semitism.

The considerations up to this point give rise to a justifiable assumption: Heidegger's being-historical Manichaeism, which increases at the end of the 1930s, his narrative of a history of the world and the homeland threatened by the un-history of worldlessness and homelessness (*Heimatlosigkeit*), formed a milieu in which his anti-Semitism, long latent to be sure, could now take on its own being-historical significance. In this context, deceptive stories (the *Protocols of the Elders of Zion*) and simpleminded legends (of a Jewish "gift for calculation," for example) enter Heidegger's thinking forcibly and start to proliferate there.

One must not be deceived: Although we do not know what Heidegger intimated by the "production of corpses in the gas chambers and extermination camps" or still less what he knew, and even if we believe him that "hundreds of thousands" were "*unobtrusively* liquidated in annihilation camps," all of this still implies a central thought of his being-historical anti-Semitism: that the Jews were a military enemy of the National Socialists or, worse yet, of the Germans.[1] In the war between such enemies, at what point would Heidegger have limited the violence against the Jews? In his eyes, what was the scope of the above-mentioned "predetermination" for "planetary master criminals"? Was the "fabrication of corpses" really unthinkable when it came to an enemy, perhaps even *the* enemy? Not that Heidegger had wanted the war. Indeed while it lasted, he held it for an unavoidable step in the "overcoming of metaphysics."

Heidegger did not judge the public capable of thinking through philosophical problems of significance. This reservation may be understandable, but only under the assumption that the public is never primarily concerned with the truth. Even the *Black Notebooks*, these apparently most intimate texts of Heidegger's, keep silent about the human suffering of the Shoah. The "inability to mourn" was widespread, certainly not in conservative circles alone.[2] Thus Heidegger could speak with great feeling about mourning and pain, and nevertheless write in the *Bremen Lectures*: "Everywhere we are assailed by innumerable and measureless suffering. We, however, are unpained, not brought into the ownership of the essence of pain."[3] Did he possibly mean himself, or at least others including himself? In such an admission, can we not hear at least an echo of his having been affected? But the inability to experience "the essence of pain," according to his view, lies in the presumptions of modern technology, not in the indifference of one's own emotionality.

The lack of testimony for any mourning over the "innumerable and measureless suffering" is conspicuous in such an inflationary testament of mourning over being-historical "homelessness."[4] Indeed let us assume for a moment that the philosopher actually would have been completely immune to the pain that ensues in regard to the Shoah; would the reunion with Hannah Arendt then not be completely incomprehensible, indeed, even unbelievable? Must not Arendt herself have been certain that this dear man had experienced the pain? Not that she had directly burdened him with the "log" of it, but it is unthinkable that Arendt would accept her beloved's remaining cold before the crimes of the Germans. Admittedly, we are here left only with conjecture.[5]

There is a being-historical anti-Semitism in Heidegger that appears to contaminate not just a few dimensions of his thinking. This fact throws a new light on Heidegger's philosophy as well as its reception. If previously Heidegger's involvement with National Socialism was a problem that led in part to exaggerated condemnations and in part to justified reservations, then with the publication of the *Black Notebooks*, the presence of a specific anti-Semitism—which arises at a time when the thinker very critically confronted real, existing National Socialism—cannot be overlooked.

The philosophical and academic engagement with Heidegger in years ahead will work at drawing the consequences of this now philologically indubitable state of affairs. One need not be a prophet to foresee an institutional crisis in the reception of Heidegger's thinking. The question whether the anti-Semitic passages of the *Black Notebooks* prompt a necessary leave-taking from Heidegger's thinking as a whole is not at all irrelevant. Whoever will philosophize with Heidegger must be clear about the anti-Semitic implications of certain specific traits of his thought.

From now on, any attempt to isolate the being-historical anti-Semitism in Heidegger's texts so as to distinguish "anti-Semitism-free" zones in his thinking will be regarded as scandalous. The contamination does not begin only in the thinking of the 1930s, nor is it subsequently restricted to that. Are there fundamental decisions in Heidegger's philosophy that provide an opening from the outset for the adoption of a being-historical enemy? Does the characteristic and often fascinating radicality of this thinking overshoot the aim of philosophizing when it desires a "purification *of being*"? Is *this* radicality the origin of being-historical anti-Semitism?

The anti-Semitic contamination of Heidegger's thinking— how far does it reach? Does it affect the corpus of this thinking as a whole? Does it seize the history of being and being-historical thinking alone? Can it even be delimited? I have already indicated that I hold Heidegger's being-historical anti-Semitism to be the consequence of a being-historical Manichaeism, which at the end of the 1930s came to a full outburst and drove his thinking into an either/or from which the Jews and their destiny were not spared. As Heidegger's narrative of the German salvation of the West—the yearning for a "purification *of being*"—fell into a crisis, the Jews emerged on the side of the enemy. The limits of the contamination of Heidegger's text coincide with the limits of this being-historical *Manichaeism*. To the degree that "beyng" and "beings" were no longer alternatives, as reflected in the alternatives of "other beginning" and "machination," the possibility vanished for the hypostatization of a hostile "world Judaism." To speak of a being-historical anti-Semitism therefore does not imply that being-historical thinking as such is anti-Semitic.

Finally, we cannot avoid connecting the desire for a "purity *of being*" with the purity phantasmagoria that, at the very least, helped to organize one of the greatest crimes against humanity. The Nuremberg laws state that "purity of blood" is "the presupposition for the continued existence of the German people." At the end of the 1930s, Heidegger placed *this* purification on the side of the "deepest deformation of being by the precedence of beings" (for this reason he emphasizes "purity *of being*"). And, indeed, in his radicalizing of the difference between being and beings, he falls victim in his own thinking to a basic trait of the "*brutalitas* of being," i.e., the violence of "machination." The extreme of a *pure being* when it is thought as history, as location of "Da-sein," which is how Heidegger indeed thinks it, cannot escape the violence from which it attempts with all its power to remove itself. It necessarily falls prey to a counterviolence that increases all the more, the more violently it experiences the first violence.

Heidegger liberated himself from the narrative that stood

at the beginning of his radicalization of the difference between "beyng" and "beings"—slowly, to be sure, and painfully, but at last, pointedly. His thinking in his final three decades achieved a measure that he lacked in the measureless time between 1933 and 1947. The *Black Notebooks* attest to how deeply Heidegger was involved with the convulsions of the times, how much his thinking had suffered in these convulsions—not only in terms of the injury that being-historical anti-Semitism proved to be. After 1945 Heidegger interpreted many things in the way he wanted to see them—scarcely a text shows that so overtly as the *Black Notebooks*. At the same time, however, they unsparingly present an exposure of thought that Heidegger did not wish to renounce at the end of his life. Did he forget what the notebooks contained? Or did he want to let us take part in a philosophical drama unique in the German intellectual history of the twentieth century? Was not Heidegger's keeping the *Black Notebooks* secret, along with the instruction to publish them last of all, perhaps bound up with the intention of showing us just how far his—any—thinking can proceed along false paths?[6] Did not everyone close to him, i.e., relatives and friends and co-workers, advise him against their publication?

In the end, it can be said that henceforth Heidegger's thinking will present itself as a unique philosophical challenge. To arrive at this view, I do not need to refer first to the work of Heidegger, which in its ever new and surprising force of thinking belongs to that inexhaustible philosophical source where all the great texts of philosophers from Plato to Wittgenstein are gathered. For in the past century, it is not only the history of philosophy that is incomprehensible without him. Heidegger's historical effect oversteps the limits of philosophy. He will remain the philosopher who lets us remember like no other the "dark times" of the twentieth century. Admittedly he does this in an entirely different way than those "men in dark times" whom

Hannah Arendt presents in her essays—while she never refused him a place among them.[7] His involvement even in the darkest traits of that time colors the memory we receive from him. That memory is painful not only for what is remembered, but also for the sometimes horrifying way and manner of the memoir itself. And can we not feel gratitude for the fact that Heidegger's thinking never and nowhere spares us this pain, indeed this terror?

Nevertheless, the *Black Notebooks* from the 1930s and 1940s will make a revision of our confrontation with Heidegger's thinking necessary. Nothing of what has been mentioned in the back-and-forth discussions of the role of National Socialism in his thinking can compare with what the narrative of a German salvation of the West finally wrought upon this philosophy. Even if Heidegger's thinking survives that revision, the statements treated in the foregoing considerations will disfigure it like broke-open scars. A "wounding of thinking" has occurred.

Heidegger's *Überlegungen*, the first series of *Black Notebooks*, have been published and have provoked an extraordinary media response. The reactions were overwhelmingly negative. But the philosophical and academic confrontation is still to be had. What is already certain is that with this publication, Heidegger's writings enter into a new dimension, one that will entail changes in the context of his writings as a whole. Above all, the being-historical treatises—*Contributions to Philosophy (Of the Event)*, *Mindfulness*, etc.—will have to be read in parallel with the *Überlegungen*, especially since those treatises constantly refer to the *Überlegungen*.

The reaction of the international media—and is there not a strange cleft between the public and academic importance of Heidegger here?—is likewise tied to discussion of Heidegger's statements directed against the Jews, i.e., his anti-Semitic statements. Here we discern differing interpretations. I would like to point out two of these and assess their coherence.

The historical view of Heidegger's statements contextualizes them and establishes that they remain far behind the most prominent forms of anti-Semitism of the Third Reich. In fact, the anti-Semitism that I characterize as being-historical simply cannot be compared with anti-Semitism à la Julius Streicher.[1] Moreover, Heidegger kept his statements secret. He played no role in the anti-Semitic milieu of the Third Reich. These historical reminders are not unimportant, but must be distinguished from a philosophical interpretation. This is already the case, because Heidegger lets his statements on "world Judaism" surface in a philosophical context. Finally, what is problematic in this position cannot be resolved by referring to something still more problematic.

The second view proclaims that the passages in question belong to a grandly envisioned "culture critique." So it would be more or less natural that in a critique of "Americanism" and of "Bolshevism," of "nationalism" and of "imperialism," etc., "world Judaism" would also be named. Insofar as history vanishes into an end situation of total "machination," everything falls under its (machination's) dominance. Since "world Judaism" would have a special relation to technology and its economy (owing to its "marked gift for calculation"), it would prove to be as much the master of this dominance as its slave. I skeptically oppose this interpretation. If someone were to proclaim today that the Chinese are particularly suited for global capitalism because they are capable of an entirely non-European personal self-renunciation, indeed of self-enslavement, we would most likely not hold that for a sensible critique of capitalism. The characterization would lead to outrage and rightly so.

Additionally, I have been criticized for the thesis that Heidegger's anti-Semitism was influenced by, if not stamped by, the *Protocols of the Elders of Zion*. It was and is objected that Heidegger had not read the *Protocols*, did not know of them. This pseudo-philological objection assumes that only a person who had read Hitler's *Mein Kampf* was a National Socialist. With this, one would quickly reduce the number of National Socialists in the Third Reich to a handful. I do not claim that Heidegger had read the *Protocols of the Elders of Zion*. But anyone who had heard (of) Hitler's speeches, for example, stood under their influence.

Thus I think that the concept of being-historical anti-Semitism still performs a heuristic duty.[2] It is to be set aside and shelved (*ad acta*) only when another, better interpretation of a passage arises. What I mean is that the term "green bird" lets us conclude only that we see a bird with green feathers, not that everything green we see must be a bird. Similarly, the reference to a *being-historical* anti-Semitism in Heidegger does not mean that the history of being as such is anti-Semitic.

In a certain regard, I would like to criticize myself. The concept of "contamination" conforms to a logic of purification, one that perhaps has entered my text through Heidegger's idea of a "purification of being." Here and there I have even allowed my own thoughts to be "contaminated." A poisoned thinking becomes weak, goes blind. Have I consequently overinterpreted Heidegger's statements on world Judaism? I have understood the concept of "contamination" literally, in the sense of a reciprocal touching, reciprocal grasping. When Heidegger, for whatever reason, allowed his thinking to get caught in the clutches of an imaginary threat of "world Judaism," what was touched by this presumed threat? It is this logic of purification, of cleansing, from which all thinking must be unconditionally protected—without this protection itself being understood in terms of purity.

It would certainly be desirable if, in the future, the focus fell upon the philosophical problems that we encounter in the *Black Notebooks* from the end of the 1930s. It seems to me that we are poised for a discussion of Heidegger's radical anti-universalism. The universalistic—the planetary—appears for Heidegger to be grounded solely and entirely in the technological-mathematical-scientific character of modernity. Its effect is destructive for all particulars or singularities. The possibility of a being-historical "homeland" (cf. *GA* 73.1: 753–65) is annihilated by such a universalism. Obviously, Heidegger would have to refine this relation to technology, to the universalistic as such. The thinking of "positionality" (*Ge-Stells*) provides a more sensible relation to it.

It is the Shoah that marks every confrontation with anti-Semitic ideas before 1945 with an asymmetry. Between the years 1938 and 1941, what *we* know, Heidegger did not know. He kept his *Überlegungen* secret at a time when everyone could sling anti-Semitic discourse. Anti-Semitism was a career. Thus a hermeneutic sense of justice should reign here. Indeed precisely this would have to aver that Heidegger noted down his statements on "world Judaism" while the synagogues in Germany burned. And it would have to be conceded that even in the *Black Notebooks*, those esoteric manuscripts, while many words of mourning over the suffering of the Germans are to be found, there are none concerning that of the Jews. There reigns here a silence that will long resound in our ears.

Nevertheless, this silence cannot be the last word. Philosophy is, when it happens, free. To freedom there belongs the danger of failure: "for all essential thinking needs the freedom to err, a long useless errancy" (*GA* 95: 227). Despite everything problematic entered in the *Überlegungen*, this unreasonable demand still stands. Does the drama of philosophy not consist in the possibility of error? There is perhaps no philosophy without a pain all its own.

April 20, 2014, P.T.

When *Contributions to Philosophy* was published in 1989, our understanding of Heidegger's thinking began to change. The thought of the "event" (*Ereignis*) started a trend among philosophers. Even academic research pursued this development, if somewhat reluctantly.

In 2014 a similar transformation took place. The publication of the *Black Notebooks* have initiated a discussion about Heidegger that, to be sure, will influence our dealings with his thinking even more strongly than the publication of *Contributions to Philosophy*.

The upheaval brings more good with it than bad. We are confronted with a problem that no one can ignore. The recognition of this problem—paradoxically, in a certain respect—will lead to a new freedom in Heidegger interpretation. The time when a Heidegger reading could pursue a mere reconstruction of his path of thought has faded. For reconstruction is simply immune to such a problem.

But can I proclaim that the discussions of Heidegger's anti-Semitism have brought new life to this thinking? Certainly no one can underestimate the consequences of these statements. There are enemies of philosophy who would dearly like to hinder the effect of Heidegger's thinking—already a futile attempt since it falls into a performative contradiction with itself, constantly having to remember to forget Heidegger. But even neutral readers will remain cautious.

Nevertheless, something has happened. With the publication of the *Black Notebooks* Heidegger has once again—or perhaps really for the first time—written himself into the painful history of the Shoah. Even he could not escape from this. The sorrow over the loss meets up with the terror of a thinking that does not know *this* sorrow. So long as there are humans, there are these "trails of tears."[1]

January 20, 2015, P.T.

ABBREVIATIONS

////////////////////////////

All citations to *GA* refer to Martin Heidegger, *Gesamtausgabe* (Frankfurt am Main: Vittorio Klostermann, 1976–).

GA 2	*Sein und Zeit.* Ed. Friedrich-Wilhelm von Herrmann. 1977.
GA 7	*Vorträge und Aufsätze.* Ed. Friedrich-Wilhelm von Herrmann. 2000.
GA 9	*Wegmarken.* 2nd ed. Ed. Friedrich-Wilhelm von Herrmann. 1996.
GA 11	*Identität und Differenz.* Ed. Friedrich-Wilhelm von Herrmann. 2006.
GA 14	*Zur Sache des Denkens.* Ed. Friedrich-Wilhelm von Herrmann. 2007.
GA 16	*Reden und andere Zeugnisse eines Lebensweges.* Ed. Hermann Heidegger. 2000.
GA 24	*Die Grundprobleme der Phänomenologie.* 3rd ed. Ed. Friedrich-Wilhelm von Herrmann. 1997.
GA 26	*Metaphysische Anfangsgründe der Logik im Ausgang von Leibniz.* 2nd ed. Ed. Klaus Held. 1990.
GA 34	*Vom Wesen der Wahrheit: Zu Platons Höhlengleichnis und "Theätet."* 2nd ed. Ed. Hermann Mörchen. 1997.
GA 35	*Der Anfang der abendländischen Philosophie: Auslegung des Anaximander und Parmenides.* Ed. Peter Trawny. 2012.

GA 36/37   *Sein und Wahrheit: 1. Die Grundfrage der Philosophie; 2. Vom Wesen der Wahrheit.* Ed. Hartmut Tietjen. 2001.

GA 38   *Logik als die Frage nach dem Wesen der Sprache.* Ed. Günter Seubold. 1998.

GA 40   *Einführung in die Metaphysik.* Ed. Petra Jaeger. 1983.

GA 41   *Die Frage nach dem Ding. Zu Kants Lehre von den transzendentalen Grundsätzen.* Ed. Petra Jaeger. 1984.

GA 46   *Zur Auslegung von Nietzsches II. Unzeitgemäßer Betrachtung.* Ed. Hans-Joachim Friedrich. 2003.

GA 53   *Hölderlins Hymne "Der Ister."* 2nd ed. Ed. Walter Biemel. 1993.

GA 55   *Heraklit: 1. Der Anfang des abendländischen Denkens. 2. Logik: Heraklits Lehre vom Logos.* 3rd ed. Ed. Manfred S. Frings. 1994.

GA 58   *Grundprobleme der Phänomenologie (1919/20).* Ed. Hans-Helmuth Gander. 1993.

GA 60   *Phänomenologie des religiösen Lebens: 1. Einleitung in die Phänomenologie der Religion; 2. Augustinus und der Neuplatonismus; 3. Die philosophischen Grundlagen der mittelalterlichen Mystik.* Ed. Matthias Jung and Thomas Regehly, and Claudius Strube. 1995.

GA 65   *Beiträge zur Philosophie (vom Ereignis).* 2nd ed. Ed. Friedrich-Wilhelm von Herrmann. 1994.

GA 66   *Besinnung.* Ed. Friedrich-Wilhelm von Herrmann. 1997.

GA 67   *Metaphysik und Nihilismus: 1. Die Überwindung der Metaphysik; 2. Das Wesen des Nihilismus.* Ed. Hans-Joachim Friedrich. 1999.

GA 69   *Die Geschichte des Seyns: 1. Die Geschichte des Seyns; 2. Κοινόν: Aus der Geschichte des Seyns.* Ed. Peter Trawny. 1998.

GA 71   *Das Ereignis.* Ed. Friedrich-Wilhelm von Herrmann. 2009.

GA 73.1   *Zum Ereignis-Denken.* Ed. Peter Trawny. 2013.

GA 73.2   *Zum Ereignis-Denken.* Ed. Peter Trawny. 2013.

GA 76   *Leitgedanken zur Entstehung der Metaphysik, der neuzeitlichen Wissenschaft und der modernen Technik.* Ed. Claudius Strube. 2009.

GA 79   *Bremen und Freiburger Vorträge: 1. Einblick in das was ist; 2. Grundsätze des Denkens.* 2nd ed. Ed. Petra Jaeger. 2005.

GA 84.1 *Seminare Kant—Leibniz—Schiller. Teil 1: Sommersemester 1931 bis Wintersemester 1935/36.* Ed. Günther Neumann. 2013.

GA 86 *Seminare Hegel—Schelling.* Ed. Peter Trawny. 2011.

GA 94 *Überlegungen* II–VI. Ed. Peter Trawny. 2014.

GA 95 *Überlegungen* VII–XI. Ed. Peter Trawny. 2014.

GA 96 *Überlegungen* XII–XV. Ed. Peter Trawny. 2014.

GA 97 *Anmerkungen* I–V. Ed. Peter Trawny. 2015.

NOTES

////////////////////////////

PREFACE TO THE ENGLISH TRANSLATION

1. Richard Wolin, "National Socialism, World Jewry, and the History of Being: Heidegger's Black Notebooks," and Donatella Di Cesare, "Heidegger, das Sein und die Juden."

2. Cf. Joachim Prinz, "Wir Juden": "The Jew, startled out of the narrow ghetto (although indeed in many regards a place more free and clear) with the swing of a great and epochal turn in the 'great age,' suffers the fate of the parvenu. His table of values breaks apart. His equilibrium is disturbed. And so he supports himself each time on what the epoch harbors of new 'values.' In place of his former instinctual certainty, he now has a 'nose' for the modern. 'Modern as a minute from now'—because he does not understand the day or the hour" (28). This book by Rabbi Prinz assembles the motives for a renunciation of the modern, a meditation upon the origin, and the grounding of a new society. Similar motives are found in Herzl and Buber. Heidegger probably would have understood them as indications of the correctness of his proclamations.

3. Friedrich Hölderlin, "Conciliator, You That No Longer Believed In . . . : Preliminary Drafts for 'Celebration of Peace,'" *Poems and Fragments*, 453.

4. Cf. Martin Heidegger, *Überlegungen* VII, 49–50, in *Überlegungen* VII–XI, *GA* 95.

5. Emmanuel Levinas, "Heidegger, Gagarin and Us."

6. Martin Heidegger, *Überlegungen* XIV, 91, in *Überlegungen* XII–XV, *GA* 96.

INTRODUCTION: A THESIS IN NEED OF REVISION

1. Jonas, *Memoirs*, 59: "Many of these young Heidegger worshippers, who'd come great distances, even from as far away as Königsberg, were Jews. That can't have been a coincidence, though I have no explanation for it. But I assume the attraction wasn't mutual. I don't know whether Heidegger felt entirely comfortable with all these Jews swarming around him, but actually he was completely apolitical." The concluding judgment concerning Heidegger as "apolitical" is simply false. In the Third Reich, Heidegger thought "more politically" than most professors. On the proximity of Heideggerian thinking and Judaism, see Zarader, *Unthought Debt*.

2. Baumann, *Erinnerungen an Paul Celan*.

3. Derrida, "Heidegger's Silence," 147. What does "wounding of thinking" (*blessure pour la pensée*) mean? (Calle-Gruber, *Conférence*, 81). What or who has struck a wound in whom? Did the "wounding" take place in Heidegger's thinking? What did it teach him? Or is Heidegger's thinking a damaging *of* thinking more generally? Is *our* thinking wounded? Indeed, is anti-Semitism on the whole a wounding of thinking? Translator's note: Derrida's text, first published in a German translation, is excerpted from his remarks at a conference in Heidelberg in 1988. The French transcript of this conference is found in Calle-Gruber, ed., *La Conférence de Heidelberg*.

4. For example, "Letter on 'Humanism,'" *Pathmarks*, 242; *GA* 9: 317.

5. Safranski, *Martin Heidegger*, 254: "Was Heidegger anti-Semitic? Certainly not in the sense of the ideological lunacy of Nazism. It is significant that neither in his lectures and philosophical writings, nor in his political speeches and pamphlets are there any anti-Semitic or racist remarks." Beyond this, see Philippe Lacoue-Labarthe, *Heidegger, Art and Politics*: "Heidegger overestimated Nazism and probably wrote off as merely incidental certain things which were already in evidence before 1933 to which he was, in fact, staunchly opposed: anti-semitism, ideology ('politicized science') and peremptory brutality" (21). Heidegger's thinking is no "ideology" (he scorns this), although at times it does become ideological.

6. On this problem see Benz, *Was ist Antisemitismus?*, 9–28.

7. Translator's note: the term "being-historical," *seinsgeschichtlich*, refers to Heidegger's conception of a "history of being," *Geschichte des Seins*, first pursued in the 1930s and elaborated in the "being-historical treatises," beginning with *Contributions to Philosophy (Of the Event)* of 1936–38. The term will be developed further in the following chapter.

8. The number is as follows: fourteen notebooks with the title *Überlegungen* (Considerations), nine *Anmerkungen* (Remarks), two *Vier Hefte* (Four Notebooks), two *Vigiliae*, one *Notturno*, two *Winke* (Hints), four *Vorläufiges* (Preliminaries).

9. Heidegger, *Anmerkungen* II, 77, in *Anmerkungen* II–V, *GA* 97. All citations from the *Black Notebooks* are by individual notebook name followed by page number therein. Notebook pagination is supplied in the margins of the corresponding *Gesamtausgabe* volume. Translator's note: the German *Seyn*, "beyng," is, an older spelling of *Sein* ("being")—one still found in Schelling, Hölderlin, and Hegel—and is used by Heidegger in the mid 1930s to emphasize the historical, destinal, and nonobjective character of being.

10. Cf. Zaborowski, *"Eine Frage von Irre und Schuld,"* 637: "If Heidegger actually had been an anti-Semite inwardly and of deep conviction, in the sense of the racial anti-Semitism represented by the National Socialists, then in the time from 1933 to 1945, and above all during the rectorate, he would have had ample opportunity to show this publicly and thereby to work with the new authorities." This is an argument against an "inward anti-Semitism of deep conviction." Nevertheless, we know the extent to which Heidegger tended to keep his thinking far from every form of publicity. Philosophy and publicity are mutually exclusive for him. That he secreted away his anti-Semitic ideas can also be understood from this perspective.

11. Heidegger, *Überlegungen* VI, 14. In *Überlegungen* II–VI, *GA* 94.

THE BEING-HISTORICAL LANDSCAPE

1. Heidegger, *Basic Problems of Phenomenology*, 11; *GA* 24: 15.

2. Heidegger, *Metaphysical Foundations of Logic*, 157; *GA* 26: 199.

3. I prefer the concept of "narrative" and consider that of a "remythologizing" to be unfitting. Heidegger was not interested in founding a "new mythology," even if in later manuscripts the concept of a *"mytho-logy of the event"* appears to rehabilitate such a notion (Heidegger, *Zum Ereignis-Denken* [Toward Event-Thinking], *GA* 73.2: 1277). In *Winke x Überlegungen (II) und Anweisungen*, however, it says: "The reference to some higher or highest reality—Christianity—[or even] an invented myth of any such sort—no longer helps at all, though it did for a long time." Heidegger, *Winke x Überlegungen (II) und Anweisungen*, 84, in *Überlegungen* II–VI, *GA* 94. The mentioned "mytho-logy of the event" must stand at the beginning of any thematic tracing of the narratival character of the history of being.

4. Heidegger, *Being and Time*, 436; *GA* 2: 508.
5. Heidegger, *Being and Time*, 443; *GA* 2: 516.
6. Heidegger, *Hölderlin's Hymn "The Ister,"* 143; *GA* 53: 179.
7. Heidegger, *Essence of Truth*, 7; *GA* 34: 10.
8. Heidegger, *Essence of Truth*, 62, translation modified; *GA* 34: 85.
9. Heidegger, *Mindfulness*, 374, translation modified; *GA* 66: 424. Translator's note: *Of the Event* is Heidegger's private name for *Contributions to Philosophy*.
10. Heidegger, *Der Anfang der abendländischen Philosophie. Auslegung des Anaximander und Parmenides* (The Beginning of Western Philosophy: An Interpretation of Anaximander and Parmenides), *GA* 35: 1.
11. Heidegger, *Winke x Überlegungen (II) und Anweisungen*, 89, in *GA* 94.
12. What is instated here is a metapolitics. This concept must be newly assessed in its particular significance for Heidegger. On "politics" in the NS-period for Heidegger, see Sommer, *Heidegger 1933*; Zaborowski, *"Eine Frage von Irre und Schuld?"*; Faye, *Heidegger: The Introduction of Nazism into Philosophy*; Amato et al., *Heidegger à plus forte raison*; Rockmore, *On Heidegger's Nazism and Philosophy*, as well as the important essay by Donatella di Cesare, "Heidegger, das Sein und die Juden." My essay is not conceived as a general confrontation with Heidegger's adoption of and separation from National Socialism. For me, as for di Cesare, it is an issue of anti-Semitism, certainly an important dimension of this entire context.
13. The thesis that the relation of the "first" to the "other beginning" would motivate Heidegger's thinking through to 1945 needs refining. That a manuscript such as *Contributions to Philosophy* (1936–38) is determined by this relation is significant. But in the writings after 1940, the talk of an "other beginning" disappears—if not abruptly, then increasingly. Already in the 1941–42 manuscript *The Event*, the idea is stressed differently. Indeed, at one point we read: "The experience of the beginning as downfall." Heidegger, *The Event*, 243, translation modified; *GA* 71: 280. Here the concrete experience of history asserts itself. The course of the war is threatened. The "downfall" as onto-tragic movement now becomes increasingly important.
14. Heidegger, *Die Geschichte des Seyns* (The History of Beyng), *GA* 69: 27.
15. Translator's note: Heidegger's term *Machenschaft*, "machination," names the processes that objectify the world of Dasein and that render this a matter of lived experience (*Erlebnis*). Foremost among such processes is that of modern technology. *Machenschaft* thus produces beings understood in

terms of what can be "made" (*macht*) by the power (*Macht*) of the will. The term plays a central role in *Contributions to Philosophy (Of the Event)*.

16. Cf. Trawny, *Adyton*, 94–100.

17. I am aware of the problems with this concept. Manichaeism proclaims the combative separation of two irreconcilable "principles" of darkness and light. At times, Heidegger analogously separates "beyng" from "beings" (in "beyng" there are then "beyngs" [*Seyendes*]).

18. Heidegger, *Überlegungen* XIV, 113, in *Überlegungen* XII–XV, *GA* 96.

19. Cf. Burkert, *Greek Religion*, 75–83.

20. Heidegger, *Überlegungen* X, 40. In *Überlegungen* VII–XI, *GA* 95. Cf. also Heidegger, *Überlegungen* XIII, 28, in *Überlegungen* XII–XV, *GA* 96. "And all those who belong know this one decision: which will predominate, beings or beyng."

21. Heidegger is cognizant of this problem when he writes: "How terrible can this slavery become, arising from the direct dependency into which all antagonism and struggle necessarily fall?" Heidegger, *Überlegungen* IV, 93, in *Überlegungen* II–VI, *GA* 94. Related to Heidegger's characteristic alternative between "beyng" and "beings," it can be said that "beyng" falls all the more into a dependency on "beings" the more strenuously it is separated from these. "Releasement" in this context means that Heidegger appeases the relation between "beyng" and "beings" by relaxing it.

22. Cf. the formulation by which "positionality" would be thought as the "*prelude*" (*Vorspiel*) of "the event" (*Er-eignisses*). Heidegger, *Identity and Difference*, 36–37; *GA* 11: 45–46.

23. Heidegger, *Leitgedanken zur Entstehung der Metaphysik, der neuzeitlichen Wissenschaft und der modernen Technik* (Guiding Thoughts on the Emergence of Metaphysics, Modern Science, and Contemporary Technology), *GA* 76: 363.

24. Heidegger, *Überlegungen* XI, 16–17, in *Überlegungen* VII–XI, *GA* 95.

25. The second alternative recalls the being-historical figure of the "last man," as coined by Nietzsche (cf. *Thus Spoke Zarathustra*, 17). In a certain way, there is no philosopher in the *Überlegungen* so present as Nietzsche. At times Heidegger seems to want to speak in the voice of Nietzsche, even if he attempts to outdo it.

26. Heidegger, *Winke x Überlegungen (II) und Anweisungen*, 30, in *Überlegungen* II–VI, *GA* 94.

27. "To be sure, the difficulties of generalizing, as when we say 'the Germans' and 'the Jews,' intimidate the observer. In times of conflict, however, such

all-embracing terms prove easy to manipulate; and the fact that these general categories are vulnerable to questioning has never prevented people from using them vociferously." Scholem, "Jews and Germans," 72. In the following I will spare myself the quotation marks. The reason for this is that it is still not decided whether we can entirely renounce these collective concepts. Complete individualization still requires such a general horizon against which to proceed. As long as we are unable to assume a genuine dissolution of collective identity, collective concepts such as these remain of equivocal value. The omission of quotation marks is not to contest this equivocality, but merely to increase the readability of a text that already bristles with quotations.

28. Cohen, "German and Jewish Ethos I," 180, translation modified: "*The idea of humanity in Germanism* [Deutschtum] *alone rests on the basis of an ethics . . . .* At this central point we should all once again feel the inner community between Germanism and Judaism. For the concept of humanity has its origin in the *messianism* of the Israelite prophets."

29. Domarus, *Hitler*, 1: 288. In the famed speech by Otto Wels renouncing the March 1933 empowerment law of National Socialism, he says: "The gentlemen of the National Socialist Party call the Movement they have unleashed a National and not a National Socialist Revolution." I mention this only because Heidegger, with his narrative of the two beginnings of the Greeks and the Germans, could certainly latch onto a "national" revolution more easily than a "National Socialist" one.

30. Heidegger, *Überlegungen und Winke* III, 42, 52, in *Überlegungen* II–VI, *GA* 94.

31. Heidegger, *Zum Ereignis-Denken, GA* 73.1: 848.

32. Heidegger, *Überlegungen* VII, 24, in *Überlegungen* VII–XI, *GA* 95.

33. In my opinion, this is how Heidegger's infamous remark in the *Introduction to Metaphysics* concerning "the inner truth and greatness of this movement [National Socialism] (namely the encounter between global technology and modern humanity)" is to be understood. National Socialism was necessary for the transition into the "other beginning." Cf. Heidegger, *Introduction to Metaphysics*, 213; *GA* 40: 208. Nevertheless, such a formulation already appears in the lecture course of winter semester 1934–35, *Hölderlin's Hymns "Germania" and "The Rhine."* That Heidegger at this time already conceived the full being-historical interpretation of National Socialism is improbable. At the beginning of 1935, the "inner truth and greatness of National Socialism" consisted in serving the narrative of the "first" and "other beginning" via the relation of Greeks and Germans.

34. Heidegger, *Überlegungen* XI, 76, in *Überlegungen* VII–XI, *GA* 95. That Heidegger here emphasizes the "*intellectual* reasons" can only be understood in the sense that in "1930–1934" he pursued seemingly political reasons. This, however, is without doubt already a self-interpretation that must be regarded with reservation.

TYPES OF BEING-HISTORICAL ANTI-SEMITISM

1. Heidegger, *Überlegungen* XII, 67, in *Überlegungen* XII–XV, *GA* 96.
2. Heidegger, *Überlegungen* XII, 82, in *Überlegungen* XII–XV, *GA* 96.
3. Heidegger, *Überlegungen* XIV, 121, in *Überlegungen* XII–XV, *GA* 96.
4. They do not surface here for the very first time in Heidegger's work; I refer exclusively to the *Black Notebooks*. The following statements in a seminar protocol from winter 1933–34 already provided an occasion for discussion: "For a Slavic people, the nature of our German space would definitely be revealed differently from the way it is revealed to us; to Semitic nomads, it will perhaps never be revealed at all." Heidegger, *Nature, History, State*, 56; *Über Wesen und Begriff von Natur, Geschichte und Staat*, 82. The statement touches on the important relation for Heidegger between place and self. The "earth" is not simply the globe, but rather a "rootedness" in the landscape that appears differently to each respective people. In this sense, the German landscape corresponds solely to the Germans. In terms of content, the statement just cited belongs in the realm of being-historical anti-Semitism. The word choice, however, does not entirely sound like Heidegger. The protocol was composed by Helmut Ibach, perhaps the same person as the editor Helmut Ibach, *Kleine Feldpostille: Soldatische Richtbilder aus drei Jahrtausenden* (Postcards from the Battlefield: Soldierly Paragons from Three Millennia). The *historical question* as to why being-historical anti-Semitism surfaces in the *Black Notebooks* around 1937 and then intensifies in 1939–41 is an important one, but can be answered only conjecturally. It is notable that Heidegger identifies the Jews as enemies of war. The more therefore that Germany falls into a political-military crisis—and with it, Heidegger's conception of a particular Western task for the Germans—the more frequently does Heidegger pursue anti-Semitic ways of thinking. Added to this, Heidegger's two sons, Hermann and Jörg, were increasingly engaged in military conflicts.
5. Heidegger, *Überlegungen* VIII, 9, in *Überlegungen* VII–XI, *GA* 95.
6. This thought seemingly precludes our connecting what Heidegger ascribes

to Judaism with Hegel's doctrine of a "people's spirit" or "peoples' spirits": "The concrete Ideas, the spirits of various peoples [*Völkergeister*], have their truth and determinacy in the concrete Idea insofar as this is *absolute universality*, i.e., in the world spirit, around whose throne they stand as the agents of its actualization and as witnesses and ornaments of its mastery." Hegel, *Elements of the Philosophy of Right*, 376 (§ 352), translation modified. Cf. also Hegel, *Philosophy of History*, 52–53. Since Heidegger makes "machination" the founding principle of both "calculating Judaism" and imperialistic National Socialism, he appears to escape the Hegelian relation between universal and particular. And nevertheless the structure between the "people's spirits" and the "world spirit" is retained—only that now the "world spirit" of the twentieth century is machination.

7. In a letter from Martin to Elfride Heidegger, he says in 1920: "Here there's a lot of talk about how many cattle now get bought up from the villages by the Jews. . . . the farmers are gradually getting insolent up here too & everything's swamped with Jews & black marketeers." Heidegger, *Letters to His Wife*, 77; *Mein liebes Seelchen!*, 112.

8. Cf. Martin Buber, "Sie und Wir", 157: "As is well known, the problem of the Jewish relation to the economy of the dominant peoples rests in that for the most part their participation does not begin at the foundation of the house, but rather on the second story. On the contrary, they have no share, or only a miniscule one, in primal production, in the arduous attainment of raw materials, the hard work in the soil, in agriculture as well as in mining. In the manual working over of raw materials they prefer for the most part the easier professions which can be performed while sitting, and in industrial dealings they stand as technicians, engineers, and directors and keep far from hard work on machines. As I have heard with great concern, even in Soviet Russian business not much has changed in this." Even this is a 1939 example of how general attributions were made. Buber argues not historically but rather in the context of the "life of the people." The discussion of the relation of the Jews to "primal production" appears to have a tradition. Already Theodor Herzl addressed this when he wrote: "Whoever would attempt to convert the Jew into a husbandman would be making an extraordinary mistake. For a peasant is in a historical category, as proved by his costume which in some countries he has worn for centuries; and by his tools, which are identical with those used by his earliest forefathers. . . . But we know that all this can be done by machinery. The agrarian question is only a question of machinery. America must conquer

Europe." Herzl, *Jewish State*, 87–88. Herzl combines the question of "primal production" with the meaning of technological modernity.

9. Simmel, "Deutschlands inner Wandlung," 14–16.

10. Heidegger, "Memorial Address" ("Gelassenheit"), *Discourse on Thinking*, 46, translation modified; *GA* 16: 519: "Calculative thinking calculates. It calculates ever new, ever more promising, and, at the same time, ever cheaper possibilities."

11. It can be no accident that Leo Strauss made particular reference to Heidegger's employment of the concept of "rootedness." Cf. Strauss, "Philosophy as Rigorous Science," 33.

12. Something Heidegger also knows, as when he writes: "The mathematical idea of knowledge that begins with modernity—itself at base Ancient." Heidegger, *Winke x Überlegungen (II) und Anweisungen*, 63, in *Überlegungen II–VI, GA* 94. All the more can we ask why Heidegger did not hold fast to this insight and develop it further. Translator's note: the *mathesis universalis* is a key conception of modern philosophy whereby everything is defined as a possible object for mathematics. See Heidegger, *What Is a Thing?*, 65–108; *GA* 41: 65–108.

13. In *Contributions to Philosophy*, there is a passage that appears to contradict what is presented here: "*Sheer idiocy* to say that experimental research is Nordic-Germanic and that rational research, on the contrary, is of *foreign extraction*! We would then have to resolve to number Newton and Leibniz among the 'Jews.'" Heidegger, *Contributions to Philosophy*, 127; *GA* 65: 163. The appearance is nevertheless deceptive. The expression: all "calculative thinking" is "Jewish" is not identical with the expression: all "Jewish thinking" is "calculative." The first expression Heidegger has to deny, because the great thinkers of modernity were actually not Jews. The second expression he can affirm without falling into contradiction with the first. Cf. also the previous note.

14. Heidegger, *Überlegungen* XII, 69, in *Überlegungen* XII–XV, *GA* 96.

15. Heidegger, *Überlegungen* XII, 82, in *Überlegungen* XII–XV, *GA* 96.

16. Heidegger, *Überlegungen* III, 127, in *Überlegungen* II–VI, *GA* 94.

17. Naturally it is possible to ask whether there could be a Jewish "racism." Christian Geulen, in his clever *Geschichte des Rassismus* (History of Racism), defines racism as an activity endeavoring "to theoretically ground and practically produce either conventional or new limits of belonging" (11). In this sense the author states that Judaism knows an "asymmetrical self- and foreigner image structure," though it would "in no way" aspire "auto-

matically" to "the conquest, colonization, or oppression of foreign cultures" (25). Judaism has continually made a "passive claim to exclusivity" in its "competition with the respective hegemonic cultures." It is a social-psychological question as to whether and how this "passive claim to exclusivity"—that of being the "chosen people"—can be an impetus for racist reactions to the difference that constantly presents itself between belonging and nonbelonging.

18. Cf. Alicke, *Lexikon der jüdischen Gemeinden*, col. 1306: "In the early morning hours of the 10th of November, 1938, the Freiburg synagogue on Werderring was burned down. The arsonists forced the leading men of the synagogue community to attend the burning. That same night, even the Jewish cemetery was vandalized. Even while the synagogue burned, about 140 Jewish men were arrested and on the evening of November 10 transported away to the Dachau concentration camp." It is further said that "at the end of October in 1940, a majority of the 350 Jews that remained in the city ['more than 1,100 Jews' had emigrated]—together with about 6,500 others—were deported to Gurs; most of them came here in order to stay alive or were murdered in the death camps." In 1940, Hannah Arendt found herself in the same camp, though she was able to leave in June. Cf. Young-Bruehl, *Hannah Arendt*, 153–56.

19. Cf. Heidegger, *Zur Auslegung von Nietzsches II. Unzeitgemäßer Betrachtung* (On the Interpretation of Nietzsches 2nd "Unfashionable Observation"), *GA* 46: 259–62. A note from this session runs: "This ever increasing power, which constitutes the essence of mightiness [*Mächtigkeit*], rules all claims; that is to say, violence and robbery are not consequences and ways of carrying out otherwise justified claims, but rather the reverse: robbery is the ground of justification. We still know little of the 'logic' of power, because we still constantly blend *moral* considerations into it and because the proclamation of power itself, in the interest of power, employs 'moral' reasons and goals (cf. for example, the English 'cant')" (*GA* 46: 215–16). "Cant" is a jargon that can be ascribed to various groups (religious sects, criminals, etc.).

20. Heidegger, *Überlegungen* XIV, 79–80, in *Überlegungen* XII–XV, *GA* 96.

21. Heidegger, *Überlegungen* VII, 88, in *Überlegungen* VII–XI, *GA* 95. Translator's note: these Aryan variants of psychoanalysis would include the work of the Deutsches Institut für psychologische Forschung und Psychotherapie in Berlin under the leadership of Matthias Göring, cousin of Hermann Göring, from 1936 to 1945 (the "Göring Institute").

22. Heidegger, *Überlegungen* IX, 123, in *Überlegungen* VII–XI, *GA* 95. Freud, for example, also attempted to attract the non-Jew Carl Gustav Jung to his side on "racial" grounds. He says as much in a letter to Karl Abraham: "his adherence is all the more valuable. I almost said that only his appearance has saved psychoanalysis from the danger of becoming a Jewish national concern." Cf. Gay, *Freud*, 204.

23. Jaspers, *Philosophische Autobiographie*, 101.

24. Sammons, *Die Protokolle der Weisen von Zion: Die Grundlage des modernen Antisemitismus—eine Fälschung* (The Protocols of the Elders of Zion: The Foundation of Modern Anti-Semitism—A Forgery). Cf. also on the protocols, Poliakov, *History of Anti-Semitism*, 4: 210–13, as well as Benz, *Die Protokolle der Weisen von Zion: Die Legende von der jüdischen Weltverschwörung* (The Protocols of the Elders of Zion: The Legend of a Jewish World Conspiracy).

25. Translator's note: A "forgery" is the subtitle of Sammons's annotated edition of the *Protocols*.

26. Stein, *Adolf Hitler, "Schüler der Weisen von Zion."*

27. Arendt, *Origins of Totalitarianism*, 358.

28. Ibid., 378.

29. Sammons, *Die Protokolle der Weisen von Zion*, 37.

30. Ibid., 53.

31. Baynes, *Speeches of Adolf Hitler*, 2: 1140; cf. Domarus, *Hitler*, 1: 392.

32. Cf. Domarus, *Hitler*, 3: 1449, translation modified.

33. What or who is "England"? Immediately after the passage cited above as citation 3 ("Even the thought of an agreement with England . . ."), Heidegger adds: "Why do we recognize so late that, in truth, England is and is able to exist *without* a Western bearing? Because only in the future will we grasp that England initiated the arrangement of the *modern* world, and that this modernity, in keeping with its essence, is directed at the unleashing of machination across the entire globe." Heidegger understands England as the origin of Americanism and Bolshevism, because it pursues the "unleashing of machination." At another place he writes: "What we did to the Czechs and Poles, England and France want to do to the Germans as well; only that France would like to retain its ahistoricality [*Geschichtslosigkeit*] through a destroyed Germany and England through a gigantic business; while for the *coming* Germans there is allotted the endurance of another history—for their thinking stands in the transition to mindfulness." Heidegger, *Überlegungen* XIII, 95–96, in *Überlegungen* XII–XV, *GA* 96. Without

taking this statement about England as providing an exhaustive account of Heidegger's view, the proclamation that England's interest in the destruction of Germany would concern a "gigantic business" nevertheless carries with it, *in the present context*, an anti-Semitic connotation.

34. This attribution was so widespread that it was even affirmed by Jews themselves: "The tragedy of the Jews is the tragedy of the citizenry that lives in the metropolises. The Jew is a person of the big city, more than half the Jews of the world live in big cities. . . . Accustomed to going to the water faucet and drinking from it as a matter of course, raised with the telephone, auto, and electricity, the feeling and sense for primal production is lost on him. They no longer have any inkling of wells that the parents dug out, of the painstaking path of the forefathers and of the light that God at one time produced. This fate is admittedly the fate of the European metropolises in general." Prinz, "Wir Juden," 95–96. While most Jews in the German empire around 1900 did indeed live in Berlin, the percentage share of Jews in the total population was, however, lower than in other European big cities. Cf. on these matters Zumbini, *Die Wurzeln des Bösen* (The Roots of Evil), 42–43.

35. Heidegger, *Überlegungen* XV, 17, in *Überlegungen* XII–XV, *GA* 96.

36. Heidegger, "Letter on 'Humanism,'" *Pathmarks*, 258; *GA* 9: 339: "When confronted with death, therefore, those young Germans who knew about Hölderlin lived and thought something other than what the public held to be the typical German attitude." Although this certainly holds, it must nevertheless be asked just what they could have "lived and thought."

37. Heidegger, *Überlegungen* XIII, 77, in *Überlegungen* XII–XV, *GA* 96.

38. Heidegger, *Die Geschichte des Seyns*, *GA* 69: 78.

39. This sentence is lacking in the book. It stands in the manuscript, but is not included in the transcript of Fritz Heidegger, who indeed had thus "struck it out." In keeping with the plan for an edition of the "last hand" [*letzter Hand*; the editorial policy of Heidegger's *Gesamtausgabe*], the editor and the estate executor decided at that time not to publish the sentence. In light of the *Black Notebooks*, the statement appears differently. Chronologically, anyway, it belongs entirely in the context of the other anti-Semitic passages discussed here.

40. Cf. Heidegger, *Überlegungen* XV, 119, in *Überlegungen* XII–XV, *GA* 96. There it says at one point: "The reports just published about the Bolshevik murder cellars are supposed to be horrible." Heidegger eschews saying some-

thing similar about the Germans. Moreover, he thinks that "world Judaism" occupies the key positions among the Bolsheviks.

41. Prinz, "Wir Juden," 95. Even Prinz's idea is ultimately one specific interpretation according to which in modern times, the diaspora would be the "fate" of humans in general. I would then plead that the world-changing forms of technology have nothing to do with the diaspora, and that the cosmopolitanism accompanying globalization is without precedent. Götz Aly in his study *Why the Germans? Why the Jews?: Envy, Race Hatred, and the Prehistory of the Holocaust* finds the distinction between the fundamental conservatives (among them the placid, the backward, and the homey) and the progressives (those eager to learn and the modern) to be a very important one for German anti-Semitism.

42. Arendt, *Origins of Totalitarianism*, 354.

43. Heidegger, *Überlegungen* VIII, 9, in *Überlegungen* VII–XI, *GA* 95.

44. Heidegger, *Überlegungen* XV, 10, in *Überlegungen* XII–XV, *GA* 96.

45. Heidegger, *Die Geschichte des Seyns, GA* 69: 47.

46. To proclaim an identity of "machination" and "world Judaism" would ignore, for example, the entire discussion with Ernst Jünger's understanding of "total mobilization" or the "figure of the worker." Nevertheless, in the genesis of Heidegger's thinking of technology, an anti-Semitic *ressentiment* must be considered along with this.

47. Cf. Diner, *Feindbild Amerika*, 33: "In many respects anti-Americanism can be understood as a further stage beyond that of anti-Semitism in the global hatred of Jews." At one point in *Überlegungen* XIII, Heidegger speaks of the "commercial rational calculation [*Rechenhaftigkeit*], painted over with morals, of the English-American world." Heidegger, *Überlegungen* XIII, 50, in *Überlegungen* XII–XV, *GA* 96. This would probably have to be understood in the current context as an expression of being-historical anti-Semitism.

48. Martin Heidegger, *Metaphysik und Nihilismus, GA* 67: 150.

THE BEING-HISTORICAL CONCEPT OF "RACE"

1. Geulen, *Geschichte des Rassismus*, 13.

2. Nietzsche, *Daybreak*, 149.

3. Ibid., emphasis modified. Cf. Schank, *"Rasse" und "Züchtung" bei Nietzsche*. While Nietzsche does not doubt the presence of "race," he does waver in regard to the question of their "mixing." On the one hand, he appears

to emphasize the "purity" of the "race"; on the other hand, he is of the opinion that "mixed races" would be "the source of great culture" (Nietzsche, *Nachgelassene Fragmente*, 45). It may be that the concept of race does not stem from the central discussions of biology. It is nonetheless worth noting that Charles Darwin employed the concept of "race" as something obvious. The title of his 1859 work reads: *On the Origin of Species by Means of Natural Selection, or the Preservation of Favoured Races in the Struggle of Life.* Gobineau's *Essai sur l'inégalité des races humaines*, which influenced Wagner, appeared in two volumes between 1853 and 1855. As an indication of the difficulty that the concept of "race" still implies even today, one should recall the importance of "race" in the United States Census. The social structure of the United States appears to make a renunciation of the concept of race impossible, precisely because there is, so to speak, such an "official" racism. In a situation in which the predominance of certain social groups is racially grounded, the proclamation that there will be no races is problematic.

4. Jünger, *Der Arbeiter*, 288, 309.
5. Ibid., 156.
6. Heidegger, *Logic as the Question concerning the Essence of Language*, 57, translation modified; *GA* 38: 65.
7. Heidegger, *Logic as the Question concerning the Essence of Language*, 57; *GA* 38: 65 (underlined in the transcript of the lecture).
8. Heidegger, *Logic as the Question concerning the Essence of Language*, 131, translation modified; *GA* 38: 153.
9. Heidegger, *Hegel's "Philosophy of Right," Winter Semester, 1934-35*, 175; *GA* 86: 162.
10. Today in Germany, the concept of the "racy" is applied exclusively to women and sports cars.
11. Zaborowski emphasizes that Heidegger, in his understanding of "state and people," "opportunely, even if not so often, adopted a position that, to all external appearances, is to be characterized univocally as racist" (*"Eine Frage von Irre und Schuld?,"* 420). If "racist" means that Heidegger would have derived a superiority over other peoples from the "racial" founding of the "body of the people" of the Germans, then in my view the philosopher must be acquitted of such charges of racism. A "being-historical racism," on the contrary, consists in the fact that Heidegger did not wish to renounce the concept of race in his topology of being-historical pro-

tagonists, because he believed the authentic importance of race in general would come to the fore only in a definite epoch of the history of being. More on this later.

12. Heidegger, *Being and Truth*, 201; *GA* 36/37: 263.

13. Heidegger, *Überlegungen und Winke* III, 96, in *Überlegungen* II–VI, *GA* 94.

14. Heidegger, *Überlegungen und Winke* III, 26–27, in *Überlegungen* II–VI, *GA* 94. Somewhat later: "The attuning and formative force of the project [is] the deciding" (41). Incidentally, it can be shown how Heidegger attempted to politicize the fundamental ontology of *Being and Time* around 1933 (with the concept of "care," for example), i.e., to ontologize the political, and thus to practice "metapolitics."

15. Heidegger, *Logic as the Question Concerning the Essence of Language*, 57, translation modified; *GA* 38: 65.

16. Heidegger, *Winke x Überlegungen (II) und Anweisungen*, 45, in *Überlegungen* II–VI, *GA* 94.

17. Heidegger, *Überlegungen und Winke III*, 102, in *Überlegungen* II–VI, *GA* 94.

18. Heidegger, "The Rectorate 1933/34: Facts and Thoughts" (1945), in Neske and Kettering, *Martin Heidegger*, 20, translation modified; *GA* 16: 378. With the conception of the notion of "Western responsibility" it is nevertheless to be observed that Heidegger first applied this only after the war. In the *Black Notebooks* it surfaces just after 1945 in *Anmerkungen* II. The decision to speak of the "West" (*Abend-Land*) and the "Western" (*Abendländischen*) arises from a setting aside of the narrative of the "first" and "other beginning" in regard to the Greeks and the Germans. By "Western responsibility" did Heidegger understanding anything other than the inscribing of European history into the transition from the "first" to the "other beginning"? To be sure, for Heidegger, "Europe" is not the "West." But this cannot be gone into further here. On *"people of the earth,"* see Heidegger, *Seminare Kant—Leibniz—Schiller, GA* 84.1: 338. "Earth," here, in this ambivalent usage, certainly refers not to the planet, but to the "earth" of the "conflict of world and earth."

19. Heidegger, *Überlegungen* X, 103, in *Überlegungen* VII–XI, *GA* 95.

20. Heidegger, *Überlegungen* XII, 69–70, in *Überlegungen* XII–XV, *GA* 96.

21. Heidegger, *Überlegungen* XI, 57–58, in *Überlegungen* VII–XI, *GA* 95.

22. Heidegger, *Überlegungen* V, 36–37, in *Überlegungen* II–VI, *GA* 94.

23. Cf. Trawny, *Adyton*, 78–85.

24. Heidegger, *Überlegungen* XI, 67, in *Überlegungen* VII–XI, *GA* 95.

THE FOREIGN AND THE FOREIGN

1. Heidegger, *Winke x Überlegungen (II) und Anweisungen*, 55, in *Überlegungen* II–VI, *GA* 94.
2. Heidegger, *Überlegungen IV*, 38, in *Überlegungen* II–VI, *GA* 94.
3. Heidegger, *Überlegungen IV*, 52, in *Überlegungen* II–VI, *GA* 94.
4. Heidegger, *Überlegungen und Winke III*, 96, in *Überlegungen* II–VI, *GA* 94.
5. Heidegger, *Überlegungen IV*, 102, in *Überlegungen* II–VI, *GA* 94.
6. Heidegger, *Überlegungen IV*, 46, in *Überlegungen* II–VI, *GA* 94.
7. Cf. Waldenfels, *Topographie des Fremden*, 184–207.
8. Heidegger, *Überlegungen IV*, 24, in *Überlegungen* II–VI, *GA* 94: "The effective *enactment* of *keeping silent* [Verschweigung] and fading away *as* the opening and transformation of beings with essencing beyng./This requires, however, an essential *renunciation* of speaking about keeping silent and of saying something about the essence of language as *silence* [Schweigen]—then it may be *kept silent.*"
9. Heidegger, *Überlegungen V*, 79, in *Überlegungen* II–VI, *GA* 94.
10. The treatment of the city-country relationship in Heidegger has been continually criticized, recently by Zimmermann, *Martin und Fritz Heidegger*, 60–65. Nevertheless, I myself am not entirely sure whether Heidegger's preference for the "Black Forest hut" can be taken for a mere "stylization." It is not in keeping with the matter to deny any significance to the facticity of dwelling in different landscapes.
11. Heidegger, *Überlegungen VII*, 12, in *Überlegungen* VII–XI, *GA* 95. The thought that the Germans would imitate something "foreign" is not original. It is found, for example, in the early Nietzsche. Thus at the outset of *David Strauss the Confessor and the Writer*, Nietzsche writes: "Even if we had actually ceased to imitate the French, that would still not imply that we had triumphed over them, but only that we had liberated ourselves from our subordination to them: only if we had imposed upon the French an original German culture would we legitimately be able to speak of a triumph of German Culture. Meanwhile, we can scarcely help but note that we—necessarily—remain dependent upon Paris in all matters of form, for up to the present day there has never been an original German culture." Nietzsche, *David Strauss*, 9–10. Naturally, Heidegger bitterly rejected the concept of "culture."
12. Heidegger, *Überlegungen VII*, 14, in *Überlegungen* VII–XI, *GA* 95.
13. Heidegger, *Überlegungen IX*, 1, in *Überlegungen* VII–XI, *GA* 95.

14. Heidegger, *Überlegungen* X, 101-2, in *Überlegungen* VII–XI, *GA* 95.
15. Heidegger, *Überlegungen* XIII, 64, in *Überlegungen* XII–XV, *GA* 96.
16. Heidegger, *Hölderlin's Hymn "The Ister,"* 54; *GA* 53: 67: "*That* foreign, of course, through which the return home journeys, is not some arbitrary 'foreign' in the sense of whatever is merely and indeterminately not one's own. The *foreign* that relates to the return home, that is, is one with it, is the *provenance* of such return and is that which has been at the commencement with regard to what is one's own and the homely. For Hölderlin, the Greek world is what is foreign with respect to the historical humankind of the Germans." Superfluous to say that what holds "for Hölderlin," according to Heidegger, holds "for the Germans."
17. Thus from the outset the discussion of a linguistic chauvinism in Heidegger is nonsensical. Cf. Farías, *Heidegger and Nazism*, 298-99. The thinking of being is not bound to a particular language. What the sentence "this is a table" can mean in regard to the "is" can be said in all languages (being as existence, as essence, as truth, etc.), even when these have no word for the verbal substantive "being." Another question concerns the translatability of languages. That Heidegger had a particular interest and a peculiar conception in regard to this is well known. Whatever the case, the proclamation that languages are not translatable on a "one to one" basis is no chauvinism.
18. Heidegger, "Letter on 'Humanism,'" *Pathmarks*, 258; *GA* 9: 339.
19. Heidegger, *Anmerkungen* I, 70, in *Anmerkungen* I–V, *GA* 97.

HEIDEGGER AND HUSSERL

1. Cf. more recently, *Heidegger und Husserl: Neue Perspektiven*, ed. Günter Figal and Hans-Helmuth Gander. Despite all their differences, they are still regarded as belonging together.
2. Heidegger, "My Way to Phenomenology," *On Time and Being*, 78; *GA* 14: 98.
3. Habermas, "Work and *Weltanschauung*," 142-43.
4. Cf. Husserl's marginal notes to Heidegger's *Being and Time* and *Kant and the Problem of Metaphysics* (in Husserl, *Psychological and Transcendental Phenomenology*, 258-472). Nevertheless, there is no way that it could not have been known to him to what extent Heidegger was proceeding along his own path. Their joint work on the *Encyclopedia Britannica* article speaks against his not knowing. Heidegger himself refers in a note to their "conversation in Todtnauberg" around the time of the composition of *Being and Time*, in

which the differences between the two must have intensified. Cf. Husserl, *Psychological and Transcendental Phenomenology*, 129.

5. Husserl, *Briefwechsel*, vol. 3: *Die Göttinger Schule*, 265.

6. Husserl, *Briefwechsel*, vol. 7: 15, emphasis modified. Letter to Émile Baudin.

7. Heidegger, "The *Spiegel* Interview," in Neske and Kettering, *Martin Heidegger and National Socialism*, 48; *GA* 16: 660.

8. Cf. Karl Schuhmann, "Zu Heideggers *Spiegel*-Gespräch über Husserl."

9. Husserl, "Phenomenology and Anthropology," in *Psychological and Transcendental Phenomenology*, 485–500.

10. Translator's note: Husserl's "Nachwort zu den *Ideen* I" has been translated into English as "Author's Preface to the English Edition" of *Ideas* (Boyce Gibson edition). That translation, however, omits the opening "Preliminary Remark" of the text, from which the following citations are drawn.

11. Husserl, "Nachwort," 139.

12. Ibid., 139.

13. Ibid., 140.

14. Heidegger in a letter to Husserl from October 1927: "Dear fatherly friend! I cordially thank you and your estimable wife for the days flown by in Freiburg. I really had the feeling of being an adopted son." *GA* 14: 130.

15. Heidegger, *Anmerkungen* V, 52, in *Anmerkungen* I–V, *GA* 97.

16. Heidegger, *Anmerkungen* V, 53, in *Anmerkungen* I–V, *GA* 97.

17. Is it only a rhetorical flourish that whenever Heidegger gets wind of an anti-Semitic reproach, he meets his opponent with such a politically loaded vocabulary? "Sports-palace atmosphere," "rally," "propaganda"—all this would be directed at Husserl. Is there perhaps a strategy behind this of blaming the Jews for the sordid past? I am reminded that Paul Celan, after a reading in the "Gruppe 47" at the beginning of the 1950s, was unspeakably offended when someone, perhaps Hans Werner Richter, opined that Celan read "in the cadence of Goebbels." Cited in Milo Dor, *Auf dem falschen Dampfer*, 214.

18. Heidegger, *Anmerkungen* V, 54, in *Anmerkungen* I–V, *GA* 97.

19. Heidegger, *Anmerkungen* V, 54, in *Anmerkungen* I–V, *GA* 97.

20. Cf. the discussion around Elfride Heidegger's letter to Malvine Husserl from April 29, 1933, in which Elfride—put mildly—speaks very insensitively about the consequences of the Forced Coordination laws of March and April 1933, in Zaborowski, *"Eine Frage von Irre und Schuld,"* 390–91. However, the announcement in the *Festschrift zum 550. Jubiläum der Albert-Ludwigs-Universität Freiburg* that Malvine Husserl (1860–1950), Husserl's

wife, "on the day before the deportation of all Baden Jews in 1940" chose to commit "suicide" is simply absurd. Additionally, a false birth year was invented for Heidegger, "1891." Cf. Speck, *550 Jahre*, 171.

21. Heidegger, *Überlegungen* XII, 67, in *Überlegungen* XII–XV, *GA* 96.

22. Heidegger, *Anmerkungen* V, 17, in *Anmerkungen* I–V, *GA* 97.

23. Heidegger, *Being and Time*, 262; *GA* 2: 290–91.

24. In Martin, *Martin Heidegger und das "Dritte Reich,"* 196.

25. Walter Eucken was the son of Husserl's friend Rudolf Eucken and one of the founders of the so-called "Freiburg school of national economy," an economic direction that has been characterized since 1950 as "ordoliberalism," that is, a regulated liberalism. The historian Bernd Martin characterizes Eucken as the "authentic opponent and challenger of the rector promoting National Socialist university politics," Heidegger (Martin, *Heidegger und das "Dritte Reich,"* 26). So it is no surprise that after the war Eucken did not hold himself back—he even held Heidegger's university politics themselves to be anti-Semitic. Klinckowstroem, "Walter Eucken," 73–75. It seems an utter contradiction for Heidegger to have been able to promote "National Socialist university politics" while growing increasingly isolated in his own philosophical plans for the university.

26. Cited in Martin, *Heidegger und das "Dritte Reich,"* 149.

27. Heidegger, *Letters to His Wife*, 28; *"Mein liebes Seelchen!,"* 51.

28. Eucken was obviously not present at the corresponding faculty meeting. The story "was reported" to him, as the report says. Generally, the "Report" is ambiguous concerning Heidegger's "behavior towards Jews." It becomes clear that the incriminating statements stem from Walter Eucken, above all, and also from Adolf Lampe. Thus Eucken emphasizes "according to my memory," that Heidegger "as Rector spoke in a public speech of the 'Jewish dominance in the age of philosophical systems' and of the Jews as 'foreigners.'" Exculpatory remarks stem from Gerhard Ritter, for example. To what extent university politics play a role in the motives here is hard to say. All the same, Heidegger speaks in one place "of the denunciations of Herr Lampe, the mendacity of Herr Sauer, and the deviousness and sham-holiness of Herr von Dietze," and he asks: "What is to be expected from the remaining operators; what right do these people have to pose as moralists over against the Nazis?" Heidegger, *Zum Ereignis-Denken, GA* 73.2: 1019. During the NS period, Lampe and von Dietze were active in the Christian-oppositional "Freiburg Circle," falling into custody in 1944. Eucken was married to a Jew. But even Ritter was arrested in 1944. It is

perfectly obvious that Heidegger could not get along with either the spiritual liberalism of Eucken or the basic Protestant comportment of Lampe and von Dietze.

WORK AND LIFE

1. Biemel, *Martin Heidegger*, xi.
2. Heidegger, *Basic Problems of Phenomenology, 1919/1920*, 124; *GA* 58: 162.
3. Heidegger, *Basic Problems of Phenomenology, 1919/1920*, 27; *GA* 58: 33.
4. Martin Heidegger, *Phenomenology of Religious Life*, 6-7; *GA* 60: 8.
5. Heidegger, *Letters to His Wife*, 213; *Mein liebes Seelchen!*, 264.
6. Zimmermann, *Martin und Fritz Heidegger*, 82-89.
7. Heidegger and Bauch, *Briefwechsel*, 32.
8. Rosenkranz, *Mascha Kaléko*, 177.
9. Arendt, *Origins of Totalitarianism*, 56-70.
10. Ibid., 56.
11. Ibid., 69.
12. Arendt, *Eichmann in Jerusalem*, 133.
13. Heidegger, *Überlegungen* X, 107, in *Überlegungen* VII–XI, *GA* 95. The question is thus why Heidegger emphasizes that the author of *Nathan the Wise* was a "German poet."

ANNIHILATION AND SELF-ANNIHILATION

1. Heidegger, *Überlegungen* XV, 16, in *Überlegungen* XII–XV, *GA* 96.
2. Heidegger, *Überlegungen* XII, 65, in *Überlegungen* XII–XV, *GA* 96.
3. Heidegger, *Überlegungen* XIII, 89, in *Überlegungen* XII–XV, *GA* 96. The idea of "slaves to the history of beyng" is central to Heidegger's being-historical thinking. Everything that occurs must occur, precisely because it does occur. For this reason, Heidegger even terms his thinking "*in-human* [unmenschlich]" (*GA* 69: 24). It does not revolve around "the measures and goals and incentives of the previous humanity." Thus we see why the expressions about the persecuted and annihilated Jews sound so cold.
4. Heidegger, *Überlegungen* XIV, 113, in *Überlegungen* XII–XV, *GA* 96. Cf. also p. 12 above.
5. Heidegger, *Anmerkungen* I, 26, in *Anmerkungen* I–V, *GA* 97.
6. Cf. Heraclitus, fragment 22 (B 66): πάντα γὰρ τὸ πῦρ ἐπελθὸν κρινεῖ καὶ καταλήψεται. "Fire coming on will discern and catch up with all things."

Art and Thought of Heraclitus, 83. In his wartime lecture course on Heraclitus from the summer of 1943, Heidegger succinctly states: "The planet is in flames. The essence of the human is out of joint." Heidegger, *Heraklit, GA* 55: 123.

7. Heidegger, *Being and Truth*, 72-73; *GA* 36/37: 90-91.
8. *Being and Truth*, 73; *GA* 36/37: 91. Faye says of the cited words: "That is one of the most indefensible pages of Heidegger because the struggle he describes against the enemy lying in wait at the very root of the people describes precisely, in his own characteristic language, the reality of the racial fight of Nazism and Hitlerism against the Jews assimilated to the German people, which will lead, in the course of the those years of 1933-1935, from the first anti-Semitic measures I have described as being a part of the *Gleichschaltung* to the anti-Jewish laws of Nuremberg and the *Endlösung*, or 'Final Solution.'" Faye, *Heidegger*, 168. For Faye it is clear that the "enemy" is Judaism. He interprets its concealment as a consequence of assimilation. Then he interprets the "total annihilation" in the sense of a physical annihilation, which then would be realized in the Shoah. Naturally, none of this is mentioned here. But Heidegger ventures nothing that would preclude such an interpretation of the passage. Zaborowski comments on the passage in the following way: "Precisely in the philosophical context, when the talk is of battle, one must also think of Heraclitus's word πόλεμος—battle or war—as the 'father of all things'—a word that became increasingly important for Heidegger and that thereby helped him to justify the sublimation of the real battle into a spiritual one." Zaborowski, *"Eine Frage von Irre und Schuld,"* 271. Apart from the fact that Heraclitus's dictum intends no "spiritual battle"—in this Heidegger's interpretation is justified—Zaborowski's reference remains unclear. How could there be a "total annihilation" within a "spiritual battle"? One cannot "totally annihilate" philosophical ideas and arguments. Additionally, the application of a concept like "total annihilation" within a passionate discussion, i.e., in a "spiritual battle," would be highly unusual. Nevertheless, I do not mean that here Heidegger indubitably thinks of a physical annihilation. But I do see that he apparently concedes the possibility of being able to think this. In contrast to Heidegger's "total annihilation," cf. Friedrich Nietzsche, *Human, All Too Human*, 183: "He who lives for the sake of combatting an enemy has an interest in seeing that his enemy stays alive."

9. Heidegger, *Being and Truth*, 118; *GA* 36/37: 151.
10. Cf. Rosenberg, *Myth of the Twentieth Century*, 70, translation modified:

"Since Yahweh is conceived as materially effective, in the case of Judaism a strict monotheism is interwoven with practical material adoration (materialism) and the most sterile philosophical superstition, whereby the so called Old Testament, the Talmud, and Karl Marx convey the same insights." A typical sequence of the time: Judaism = Yahweh—Monotheism—Materialism—Marxism.

11. Heidegger, *Anmerkungen I*, 29, in *Anmerkungen I–V, GA* 97.

12. Hitler, *Mein Kampf*, 666, translation modified; Mommsen, *History of Rome*, 4: 643, translation modified.

13. Heidegger, *Überlegungen* XIV, 121, in *Überlegungen* XII–XV, *GA* 96.

14. As is well known, Marx's overlooked dissertation of 1840–41 is entitled *The Difference between the Democritean and Epicurean Philosophies of Nature*. It is accordingly an anti-Semitic strategy to characterize Marx in his materialism (which is anyway a rather limited one) as a "Jew."

15. Levinas, "Heidegger, Gagarin, and Us," 232–33.

16. Ibid., 233.

17. Ibid., 234.

18. Heidegger, *Metaphysik und Nihilismus*, *GA* 67: 164.

19. Augustine, *City of God*, 327–28.

20. Heidegger, *Anmerkungen I*, 30, in *Anmerkungen I–V, GA* 97.

21. Heidegger, *Überlegungen* XIV, 18, in *Überlegungen* XII–XV, *GA* 96.

22. Heidegger, *Überlegungen* XV, 13, in *Überlegungen* XII–XV, *GA* 96.

23. Heidegger, *Anmerkungen I*, 151, in *Anmerkungen I–V, GA* 97.

24. This means that Heidegger here anticipates what he says later: "Agriculture is now a mechanized food industry, in essence the same as the production of corpses in the gas chambers and extermination camps, the same as the blockading and starving of countries, the same as the production of hydrogen bombs." Heidegger, *Bremen and Freiburg Lectures*, 27; *GA* 79: 27. Nevertheless, what is here neutrally-relatively attributed to positionality (*Ge-Stell*) is approximately eight years earlier attributed to the "Jewish." It is not easy to pose the question *why* Heidegger identifies "machination" with the "'Jewish.'" The quotation marks displace the stereotypical character of the "marked gift for calculation" from the factually existing Jew, in order to assign the whole of technology to him. With this, Judaism is the being-historical "enemy" plain and simple.

AFTER THE SHOAH

1. Heidegger, *Bremen and Freiburg Lectures*, 27, 53; *GA* 79: 27, 56. Cf. also Arendt, *Origins of Totalitarianism*, 441.
2. Jünger, *Peace*, 29.
3. Heidegger and Arendt, *Letters*, 52-53; *Briefe*, 69.
4. At this point I cannot deny myself a personal statement. It has become customary for us to adopt an indifferent attitude toward people, independent of their culture or sex or social status. Experiences arise in accordance with "political correctness" that Heidegger did not have at his disposal. As mentioned previously (see p. 27 above), before 1945 it was common to regard a German as German and a (German) Jew as a (German) Jew. Cf. also on this point the discussion about Germanism between Karl Jaspers and Hannah Arendt in their correspondence around 1933. On this, see my book *Denkbarer Holocaust: Die politische Ethik Hannah Arendts* (Conceivable Holocaust: The Political Ethics of Hannah Arendt), 165-73.
5. Heidegger, *Letters to His Wife*, 28; *Mein liebes Seelchen!*, 51. The Reich foreign minister Walther Rathenau, murdered in June 1922 for anti-Semitic reasons, writes in an essay "Höre, Israel!" ("Hear, O Israel!") (1897) that it is a "goal" of the "state, to work against the Jewification of its public essence"—and characterizes this as "justified" (37).
6. Heidegger and Arendt, *Letters*, 142; *Briefe*, 170.
7. Heidegger and Arendt, *Letters*, 75; *Briefe*, 94.
8. Heidegger and Arendt, *Letters*, 84; *Briefe*, 104.
9. Heidegger and Marcuse, "Exchange of Letters," 30-31; *GA* 16: 430-31.
10. Heidegger, *Anmerkungen* I, 151, in *Anmerkungen* I-V, *GA* 97.
11. Heidegger and Marcuse, "Exchange of Letters," 31, translation modified; *GA* 16: 431.
12. Heidegger, *Anmerkungen* II, 60, in *Anmerkungen* II-V, *GA* 97.
13. Heidegger, *Anmerkungen* V, 21, in *Anmerkungen* II-V, *GA* 97.
14. Cf. Nietzsche, *On the Genealogy of Morals*: "All that has been done on earth against 'the noble,' 'the powerful,' 'the masters,' 'the rulers,' fades into nothing compared with what the *Jews* have done against them; the Jews, that priestly people, who in opposing their enemies and conquerors were ultimately satisfied with nothing less than a radical revaluation of their enemies' values, that is to say, an act of the most spiritual revenge. For this alone was appropriate to a priestly people, the people embodying the

most deeply repressed priestly vengefulness" (33–34). Heidegger, with his idiosyncratic hypostatization of a "spirit of revenge" proceeding against the Germans, can certainly call upon Nietzsche's moral genealogy. Doing so also casts a light back upon Nietzsche's anti-Semitism, which does not disappear when the philosopher in other passages adores the "race" of the Jews and gives free rein to his rage against anti-Semites. The thesis is probably not untenable that the (Christian-) conservative strand of German philosophical-history as a whole, from German Idealism, through Nietzsche, and on to Ernst and Friedrich-Georg Jünger, Carl Schmitt, and Martin Heidegger, was more or less latently anti-Semitic. Nevertheless, it is a matter of observing the distinctions between these kinds of anti-Semitisms.

15. Heidegger and Arendt, *Letters*, 82; *Briefe*, 101–2. I cite only a portion of the poem.

16. "Und vieles/Wie auf den Schultern eine/Last von Scheitern ist/Zu behalten. Aber bös sind/Die Pfade." Friedrich Hölderlin, "Mnemosyne," third version, *Poems and Fragments*, 518–19, translation modified. The "Scheit" is a wooden log. "Log" (*Scheit*) is related to the verb "to cut" (*scheiden*). "Scheitern" here in Hölderlin is the plural of "log" (cf. *Scheiterhaufen*, pyre, bonfire).

17. Arendt, *Denktagebuch*, 3.

18. Arendt and Jaspers, *Correspondence*, 48.

19. Heidegger and Arendt, *Letters*, 304–5; *Briefe*, 382–83.

20. Heidegger, *Anmerkungen II*, 77, in *Anmerkungen II–V, GA* 97. It is conspicuous that Heidegger does not even once regard Judaism as a religion. This holds not only for the *Black Notebooks*, but rather for his work as a whole. One exception is found in the "Letter to a Young Student," in which the philosopher speaks of the "default of god and the divinities." This manner of "absence" would be "not nothing," but rather "the presence, which must first be appropriated, of the hidden fullness . . . of what has been," under which he understands "the divine in the world of the Greeks, in prophetic Judaism, in the preaching of Jesus." Heidegger, *Poetry, Language, Thought*, 182; *GA* 7: 185. The expression sounds conciliatory; its center of gravity, however, lies in that it concerns the "fullness of what has been." When in the *Black Notebooks* the talk is of an "'eternal people,'" Heidegger means not the Jews but instead the Germans (in his "Eighth Speech to the German Nation," Johann Gottlieb Fichte contemplates the relation between a

people and eternity). An obstacle to approaching Judaism as a religion for Heidegger was certainly its significance for Christianity.

21. Another way of approaching Heidegger's being-historical anti-Semitism is that of an idiosyncratic affinity. Thus he says at one point: "Ethnology [*Volkskunde*] of whatever kind or extent never finds the 'eternal people' if those individuals of essential questioning and speaking are not first assigned to this, the ones who seek the god of the people and who throw the decision for or against this god right into the essential center of this people." Heidegger, *Überlegungen* XI, 83, in *Überlegungen* VII–XI, *GA* 95. Let us keep the possibility open for a few moments that this "god" who would have to be thrown into the "essential center of this people" would have something to do with the "last god." This would offer the opportunity, starting from this thought, to cast a glance at Judaism. The thinking of the "last god" as the nonuniversalist god of a people, a thinking that at times is to be characterized as thoroughly messianic, sounds somewhat similar to the way God is conceived in Judaism (this is an entirely preliminary pronouncement). Did Heidegger not see the Germans as a "chosen people"? How does the "last god" stand in relation to this "chosenness"? Is there in Heidegger an unacknowledged proximity to Judaism? And if there were such a proximity, what would it mean for his being-historical anti-Semitism? Cf. on all of this, Heidegger, *Contributions to Philosophy (Of the Event)*, 316; *GA* 65: 399.

22. Heidegger, *Anmerkungen* V, 10, in *Anmerkungen* I–V, *GA* 97.

23. At one point in the *Anmerkungen*, Heidegger says: "But it would be necessary that someday someone consider my anti-Christianity at least once and give it even one thought. This should not happen, so as to tolerate my thinking as still possibly "Christian." I am not a Christian, and solely because I cannot be one. I cannot be one because I, spoken in a Christian manner, do not have grace. I will never have it so long as thinking expects something of my path." Heidegger, *Anmerkungen* II, 138, in *Anmerkungen* I–V, *GA* 97. In point of fact, in the interpretation of Heidegger's thinking, the position has stubbornly persisted for decades that Heidegger's deliberations regarding, for example, the "last god" (and the "gods") can still be understood in a "Christian" manner. It would have been Christian to regard them as targeted blasphemies.

24. Heidegger, *Anmerkungen* IV, 62, in *Anmerkungen* I–V, *GA* 97.

25. Heidegger, *Anmerkungen* I, 30, in *Anmerkungen* I–V, *GA* 97.

26. Cf. Leo Strauss, "Reason and Revelation."
27. Cf. Jan Assmann, *Herrschaft und Heil.*

ATTEMPTS AT A RESPONSE

1. Heidegger, *Bremen and Freiburg Lectures*, 27, 53, emphasis modified; *GA* 79: 27, 56. Similar sounding would be Heidegger's remarks in the letter to Marcuse that "the bloody terror of the Nazis in point of fact had been kept a secret from the German people." Cf. Heidegger and Marcuse, "Exchange of Letters," 31; *GA* 16: 431.
2. Mitscherlich and Mitscherlich, *Inability to Mourn.*
3. Heidegger, *Bremen and Freiburg Lectures*, 54; *GA* 79: 57.
4. Heidegger, *Zum Ereignis-Denken*, *GA* 73.1: 819: "Nostalgia [*das Heimweh*] is the original mourning [*Urtrauer*]." The text from which this statement is drawn was composed around 1945.
5. Worthy of mention is, nonetheless, Heidegger's encounter with the Auschwitz-surviving psychoanalyst Viktor Frankl in Vienna and in Freiburg at the end of the 1950s. Cf. Frankl, *Recollections*, 113. Unfortunately, Frankl does not communicate there what was spoken between the two. Even here we might ask whether this encounter is at all conceivable without a conversation about these events. Frankl had given Heidegger the book in which he recalls his time in Auschwitz, . . . *trotzdem Ja zum Leben sagen: Drei Vorträge (Man's Search for Meaning).* So far, it has not been found in Heidegger's literary remains.
6. Cf. Trawny, *Freedom to Fail.*
7. Arendt, *Men in Dark Times.*

AFTERWORD TO THE GERMAN SECOND EDITION

1. Translator's note: Julius Streicher (1885–1946), virulently anti-Semitic National Socialist publisher and promulgator of anti-Semitic propaganda, executed at Nuremberg.
2. In the meantime, *Anmerkungen* I, which was thought missing just a short while ago, is now at hand. Silvio Vietta, in whose possession this *Black Notebook* was located, says in *Die Zeit* of January 23, 2014: "In my *Black Notebook*, there is not a single sentence against Jews, not a single anti-Semitic word" (Cammann, "Vermisstes Werk von Heidegger," 40). On the basis of my interpretation, I must beg to differ.

AFTERWORD TO THE GERMAN THIRD EDITION

1. Paul Celan, *Selected Poems and Prose*, 389: "Don't write yourself/in between the worlds,//rise up against/multiple meanings//trust the trail of tears/and learn to live."

BIBLIOGRAPHY

////////////////////////////

I. WORKS BY MARTIN HEIDEGGER IN GERMAN

Gesamtausgabe. Frankfurt am Main: Vittorio Klostermann, 1976–.

"Mein liebes Seelchen!" Briefe Martin Hedieggers an seine Frau Elfride 1915–1970. Ed. Gertrud Heidegger. Munich: Deutsche Verlags-Anstalt, 2005.

Über Wesen und Begriff von Natur, Geschichte und Staat. Übung aus dem Wintersemester 1933/34. In *Heidegger und der Nationalsozialismus. Dokumente. Heidegger-Jahrbuch* 4. Ed. Alfred Denker and Holger Zaborowski. 53–88. Freiburg: Karl Alber Verlag, 2009.

Heidegger, Martin, and Hannah Arendt. *Briefe 1925 bis 1975 und andere Zeugnisse.* Ed. Ursula Ludz. Frankfurt am Main: Klostermann Verlag, 1998.

Heidegger, Martin, and Kurt Bauch. *Briefwechsel 1932–1975.* Ed. Almuth Heidegger. Freiburg: Karl Alber Verlag, 2010.

II. MARTIN HEIDEGGER IN ENGLISH TRANSLATION

The Basic Problems of Phenomenology. Trans. Albert Hofstadter. Revised ed. Bloomington: Indiana University Press, 1988.

Basic Problems of Phenomenology: Winter Semester 1919/1920. Trans. Scott Campbell. New York: Bloomsbury, 2013.

Being and Time. Trans. John Macquarrie and Edward Robinson. San Francisco: Harper and Row, 1962.

Being and Truth. Trans. Gregory Fried and Richard Polt. Bloomington: Indiana University Press, 2010.

Bremen and Freiburg Lectures: "Insight into That Which Is" and "Basic Principles of Thinking." Trans. Andrew J. Mitchell. Bloomington: Indiana University Press, 2012.

Contributions to Philosophy (Of the Event). Trans. Richard Rojcewicz, and Daniela Vallega-Neu. Bloomington: Indiana University Press, 2012.

Discourse on Thinking. Trans. John M. Anderson and E. Hans Freund. New York: Harper, 1966.

The Essence of Truth: On Plato's Cave Allegory and "Theaetetus." Trans. Ted Sadler. New York: Continuum, 2007.

The Event. Trans. Richard Rojcewicz. Bloomington: Indiana University Press, 2013.

Hegel's "Philosophy of Right," Winter Semester, 1934-35. Trans. Andrew J. Mitchell. In *On Hegel's "Philosophy of Right": The 1934-35 Seminar and Interpretive Essays,* ed. Michael Marder, Marcia Cavalcante Schubak, and Peter Trawny. 95-200. New York: Bloomsbury, 2014.

Hölderlin's Hymn "The Ister." Trans. William McNeill and Julia Davis. Bloomington: Indiana University Press, 1996.

Identity and Difference. Trans. Joan Stambaugh. Chicago: University of Chicago Press, 2002.

Introduction to Metaphysics. Trans. Gregory Fried and Richard Polt. New Haven, CT: Yale University Press, 2000.

Letters to His Wife: 1915-1970. Ed. Gertrud Heidegger. Trans. R. D. V. Glasgow. Malden, MA: Polity Press, 2010.

Logic as the Question concerning the Essence of Language. Trans. Wanda Torres Gregory and Yvonne Unna. Albany: State University of New York Press, 2009.

The Metaphysical Foundations of Logic. Trans. Michael Heim. Bloomington: Indiana University Press, 1992.

Mindfulness. Trans. Parvis Emad and Thomas Kalary. New York: Continuum, 2006.

Nature, History, State, 1933-1934. Ed. and trans. Gregory Fried and Richard Polt. New York: Bloomsbury, 2013.

On Time and Being. Trans. Joan Stambaugh. New York: Harper & Row, 1972.

Pathmarks. Ed. William McNeill. Cambridge: Cambridge University Press, 1998.

The Phenomenology of Religious Life. Trans. Matthias Fritsch and Jennifer Anna Gosetti-Ferencei. Bloomington: Indiana University Press, 2004.

Poetry, Language, Thought. Ed. and trans. Albert Hofstadter. New York: Harper-Collins, 2001.

What Is a Thing? Trans. W. B. Barton Jr. and Vera Deutsch. Chicago: Henry Regnery, 1967.

Heidegger, Martin, and Hannah Arendt. *Letters: 1925–1975.* Ed. Ursula Ludz. Trans. Andrew Shields. Orlando, FL: Harcourt, 2004.

Heidegger, Martin, and Herbert Marcuse. "An Exchange of Letters." Trans. Richard Wolin. *New German Critique* 53 (1991): 28–32.

III. WORKS BY OTHER AUTHORS

Alicke, Klaus-Dieter. *Lexikon der jüdischen Gemeinden im deutschen Sprachraum.* Vol. 1. Gütersloh: Gütersloher Verlagshaus, 2008.

Aly, Götz. *Why the Germans? Why the Jews?: Envy, Race Hatred, and the Prehistory of the Holocaust.* Trans. Jefferson Chase. New York: Metropolitan Books, 2014.

Amato, Massimo, et al., *Heidegger à plus forte raison.* Paris: Éditions Fayard, 2007.

Arendt, Hannah. *Denktagebuch 1950 bis 1973.* Vol. 1. Ed. Ursula Ludz and Ingeborg Nordmann. Munich: Piper Verlag, 2002.

———. *Eichmann in Jerusalem: A Report on the Banality of Evil.* New York: Penguin Books, 1992.

———. *Men in Dark Times.* San Diego: Harcourt Brace, 1993.

———. *The Origins of Totalitarianism.* New edition. San Diego: Harcourt, 1994.

Arendt, Hannah, and Karl Jaspers. *Correspondence: 1926–1969.* Ed. Lotte Köhler and Hans Saner. Trans. Robert Kimber and Rita Kimber. New York: Harcourt Brace Jovanovich, 1992.

Assmann, Jan. *Herrschaft und Heil: Politische Theologie in Ägypten, Israel und Europa.* Munich: Hanser Verlag, 2000.

Augustine. *The City of God against the Pagans.* Ed. and trans. R. W. Dyson. Cambridge: Cambridge University Press, 1998.

Baumann, Gerhart. *Erinnerungen an Paul Celan.* Frankfurt am Main: Suhrkamp Verlag, 1986.

Baynes, Norman H., ed. *The Speeches of Adolf Hitler: April 1922–August 1939.* 2 vols. London: Oxford University Press, 1942.

Benz, Wolfgang. *Die Protokolle der Weisen von Zion: Die Legende von der jüdischen Weltverschwörung.* Munich: C. H. Beck, 2011.

———. *Was ist Antisemitismus?* Munich: C. H. Beck, 2004.

Biemel, Walter. *Martin Heidegger: An Illustrated Study.* Trans. J. L. Mehta. New York: Harcourt Brace Jovanovich, 1976.

Breeur, Roland, ed. "Randbemerkungen Husserls zu Heideggers *Sein und Zeit* und *Kant und das Problem der Metaphysik*." *Husserl Studies* 11 (1994): 3–63.

Buber, Martin. "Sie und Wir." In Schulte, *Deutschtum und Judentum*, 154–61.

Burkert, Walter. *Greek Religion: Archaic and Classical.* Trans. John Raffan. Cambridge, MA: Harvard University Press, 1985.

Calle-Gruber, Mireille, ed. *La conférence de Heidelberg: Heidegger, portée philosophique et politique de sa pensée.* Paris: Ligne, 2014.

Cammann, Alexander. "Vermisstes Werk von Heidegger aufgetaucht." *Die Zeit*, January 23, 2014.

Celan, Paul. *Selected Poems and Prose of Paul Celan.* Ed. and trans. John Felstiner. New York: Norton, 2001.

Cohen, Hermann. "The German and Jewish Ethos I." In *Reason and Hope: Selections from the Jewish Writings of Hermann Cohen*, ed. and trans. Eva Jospe, 176–84. New York: W. W. Norton, 1971.

Darwin, Charles. *On the Origin of Species: A Facsimile of the First Edition.* Cambridge, MA: Harvard University Press, 1964.

Derrida, Jacques. "Heidegger's Silence." Trans. Joachim Neugroschel. In Neske and Kettering, *Martin Heidegger and National Socialism*, 145–48.

Di Cesare, Donatella. "Heidegger, das Sein und die Juden." *Information Philosophie* 2 (2014): 8–21.

Diner, Dan. *Feindbild Amerika: Über die Beständigkeit eines Ressentiments.* Munich: Propylaen Verlag, 2002.

Domarus, Max. *Hitler: Speeches and Proclamations 1932–1945*, vol. 1: *The Years 1932 to 1934.* Trans. Mary Fran Gilbert. Wauconda, IL: Bolchazy-Carducci, 1990.

———. *Hitler: Speeches and Proclamations 1932–1945*, vol. 3: *The Years 1939 to 1940.* Trans. Chris Wilcox. Wauconda, IL: Bolchazy-Carducci, 1997.

Dor, Milo. *Auf dem falschen Dampfer: Fragmente einer Autobiographie.* Vienna: Zsolnay Verlag, 1988.

Farías, Victor. *Heidegger and Nazism.* Ed. Joseph Margolis and Tom Rockmore. Trans. Paul Burrell, Dominic Di Bernardi, and Gabriel R. Ricci. Philadelphia: Temple University Press, 1989.

Faye, Emmanuel. *Heidegger: The Introduction of Nazism into Philosophy.* Trans. Michael B. Smith. New Haven, CT: Yale University Press, 2011.

Fichte, Johann Gottlieb. *Addresses to the German Nation.* Ed. and trans. Gregory Moore. Cambridge: Cambridge University Press, 2009.

Figal, Günter, and Hans-Helmuth Gander, eds. *Heidegger und Husserl: Neue Perspektiven.* 2nd ed. Frankfurt am Main: Klostermann, 2013.

Frankl, Viktor. *Man's Search for Meaning.* Trans. Ilse Lasch. Boston: Beacon Press, 2006.

———. *Recollections: An Autobiography.* Trans. Joseph Fabry and Judith Fabry. New York: Insight Books, 1997.

———. *. . . trotzdem Ja zum Leben sagen: Drei Vorträge.* Vienna: Deuticke Verlag, 1946.

Gay, Peter. *Freud: A Life for Our Time.* New York: W. W. Norton, 1988.

Geulen, Christian. *Geschichte des Rassismus.* Munich: C. H. Beck, 2007.

Gobineau, Arthur de. *The Inequality of Human Races.* Trans. Adrian Collins. London: William Heinemann, 1915.

Habermas, Jürgen. "Work and *Weltanschauung:* The Heidegger Controversy from a German Perspective." Trans. John McCumber. In *The New Conservatism: Cultural Criticism and the Historians' Debate,* ed. Shierry Weber Nicholsen, 140–72. Cambridge, MA: MIT Press, 1991.

Hegel, Georg Wilhelm Friedrich. *Elements of the Philosophy of Right.* Ed. Allen W. Wood. Trans. H. B. Nisbet. Cambridge: Cambridge University Press, 1991.

———. *The Philosophy of History.* Trans. J. Sibree. New York: Dover, 1956.

Heraclitus. *The Art and Thought of Heraclitus.* Ed. and trans. Charles H. Kahn. Cambridge: Cambridge University Press, 1979.

Herzl, Theodor. *The Jewish State.* Trans. Sylvie d'Avigdor. New York: Dover, 1988.

Hitler, Adolf. *Mein Kampf.* Trans. Alvin Johnson et al. New York: Reynal and Hitchcock, 1940.

Hölderlin, Friedrich. *Poems and Fragments.* Ed. and trans. Michael Hamburger. London: Anvil Press, 1994.

Husserl, Edmund. "Author's Preface to the English Edition." In *Ideas: General Introduction to Pure Phenomenology,* trans. W. R. Boyce Gibson, 5–22. New York: Collier, 1962.

———. *Briefwechsel,* vol. 3: *Die Göttinger Schule.* Ed. Karl Schuhmann. Dordrecht: Kluwer, 1994.

———. *Briefwechsel,* vol. 7: *Wissenschaftlerkorrespondenz.* Ed. Karl Schuhmann. Dordrecht: Kluwer, 1994.

———. "Nachwort zu den *Ideen* I." In *Ideen zu einer reinen Phänomenologie und phänomenologischen Philosophie,* vol. 3: *Die Phänomenologie und die Fundamente der Wissenschaften,* 138–62. Husserliana vol. 5. Ed. Marly Biemel. The Hague: Martinus Nijhoff, 1952.

———. *Psychological and Transcendental Phenomenology and the Confrontation with*

Heidegger (1927-1931). Ed. and trans. Thomas Sheehan and Richard E. Palmer. Dordrecht: Kluwer, 1997.

Ibach, Helmut, ed. *Kleine Feldpostille: Soldatische Richtbilder aus drei Jahrtausenden*. Osnabrück: Verlag A. Fromm, 1962.

Jaspers, Karl. *Philosophische Autobiographie*. Expanded edition. Munich: Piper Verlag, 1977.

Jonas, Hans. *Memoirs*. Ed. Christian Wiese. Trans. Krishna Winston. Waltham, MA: Brandeis University Press, 2008.

Jünger, Ernst. *Der Arbeiter: Herrschaft und Gestalt*. In *Sämtliche Werke*, vol. 8: *Der Arbeiter*, 9-317. Stuttgart: Klett-Cotta, 1981.

———. *The Peace*. Trans. Stuart O. Hood. Hinsdale, IL: Henry Regnery, 1948.

Klinckowstroem, Wendula, Gräfin von. "Walter Eucken: Eine biographische Skizze." In *Walter Eucken und seine Werk: Rückblick auf den Vordenker der sozialen Marktwirtschaft*, ed. Lüder Gerken, 73-75. Tübingen: Mohr Siebeck, 2000.

Lacoue-Labarthe, Philippe. *Heidegger, Art and Politics: The Fiction of the Political*. Trans. Chris Turner. Oxford: Blackwell, 1990.

Levinas, Emmanuel. "Heidegger, Gagarin and Us." In *Difficult Freedom: Essays on Judaism*, trans. Seán Hand, 231-34. Baltimore: Johns Hopkins University Press, 1990.

Martin, Bernd, ed. *Martin Heidegger und das "Dritte Reich": Ein Kompendium*. Darmstadt: Wissenschaftliche Buchgesellschaft, 1989.

Mitscherlich, Alexander, and Margarete Mitscherlich. *Inability to Mourn: Principles of Collective Behavior*. Trans. Beverly Placzek. New York: Grove Press, 1984.

Mommsen, Theodor. *The History of Rome*. Trans. William P. Dickson. Vol. 4. New York: Charles Scribner, 1871.

Neske, Günther, and Emil Kettering, eds. *Martin Heidegger and National Socialism: Questions and Answers*. New York: Paragon House, 1990.

Nietzsche, Friedrich. *David Strauss the Confessor and Writer*. In *Unfashionable Observations*, ed. and trans. Richard T. Gray, 3-81. Stanford: Stanford University Press, 1995.

———. *Daybreak: Thoughts on the Prejudices of Morality*. Trans. R. J. Hollingdale. Cambridge: Cambridge University Press, 1988.

———. *Human, All Too Human*. Trans. R. J. Hollingdale. Cambridge: Cambridge University Press, 1989.

———. *Nachgelassene Fragmente 1885-1887*. *Kritische Studienausgabe*. Vol. 12. Ed. Giorgio Colli and Mazzino Montinari. Berlin: De Gruyter, 1988.

———. *On the Genealogy of Morals*. Trans. Walter Kaufmann and R. J. Hollingdale. In *On the Genealogy of Morals; Ecce Homo*, ed. Walter Kaufmann, 13–163. New York: Vintage Books, 1989.

———. *Thus Spoke Zarathustra: A Book for All and None*. Trans. Walter Kaufmann. New York: Penguin, 1985.

Poliakov, Léon. *The History of Anti-Semitism*. Vol. 4: *Suicidal Europe: 1870–1933*. Trans. George Klim. New York: Vanguard Press, 1965.

Prinz, Joachim. "Wir Juden." In Schulte, *Deutschtum und Judentum*, 89–115.

Rathenau, Walter, "Höre Israel!." In Schulte, *Deutschtum und Judentum*, 28–39.

Rockmore, Tom. *On Heidegger's Nazism and Philosophy*. Berkeley: University of California Press, 1992.

Rosenberg, Alfred. *The Myth of the Twentieth Century: An Evaluation of the Spiritual-Intellectual Confrontations of Our Age*. Trans. Vivian Bird. Torrance, CA: Noontide Press, 1982.

Rosenkranz, Jutta. *Mascha Kaléko: Biografie*. Munich: DTV, 2007.

Safranski, Rüdiger. *Martin Heidegger: Between Good and Evil*. Trans. Ewald Osers. Cambridge, MA: Harvard University Press, 1998.

Sammons, Jeffrey S., ed. *Die Protokolle der Weisen von Zion: Die Grundlage des modernen Antisemitismus—eine Fälschung. Text und Kommentar*. Göttingen: Wallstein Verlag, 1998.

Schank, Gerd. *"Rasse" und "Züchtung" bei Nietzsche*. Berlin: De Gruyter, 2000.

Scholem, Gershom. "Jews and Germans." Trans. Werner J. Dannhauser. In *On Jews and Judaism in Crisis: Selected Essays*, ed. Werner J. Dannhauser, 71–92. Philadelphia: Paul Dry Books, 2012.

Schuhmann, Karl. "Zu Heideggers *Spiegel*-Gespräch über Husserl." *Zeitschrift für philosophische Forschung* 32, 4 (1978): 591–612.

Schulte, Christoph, ed. *Deutschtum und Judentum: Ein Disput unter Juden aus Deutschland*. Stuttgart: Reclam Verlag, 1993.

Simmel, Georg. "Deutschlands inner Wandlung." In *Der Krieg und die geistigen Entscheidungen: Reden und Aufsätze*, 7–29. Munich: Duncker & Humblot, 1917.

Sommer, Christian. *Heidegger 1933: Le programme platonicien du Discours de rectorat*. Paris: Hermann Éditeurs, 2013.

Speck, Dieter, ed. *550 Jahre Albert-Ludwigs-Universität Freiburg*, vol. 1: *Bilder, Episoden, Glanzlichter*. Freiburg: Karl Alber Verlag, 2007.

Stein, Alexander. *Adolf Hitler, "Schüler der Weisen von Zion."* Karlsbad: Graphia, 1936.

Strauss, Leo. "Philosophy as Rigorous Science and Political Philosophy." In *Studies in Platonic Political Philosophy*, ed. Thomas L. Pangle, 29–37. Chicago: University of Chicago Press, 1983.

———. "Reason and Revelation." In Heinrich Meier, *Leo Strauss and the Theologico-Political Problem*, trans. Marcus Brainard, 141–80. Cambridge: Cambridge University Press, 2006.

Trawny, Peter. *Adyton: Heideggers esoterische Philosophie*. Berlin: Matthes & Seitz, 2010.

———. *Denkbarer Holocaust: Die politische Ethik Hannah Arendts*. Würzburg: Königshausen & Neumann, 2005.

———. *Freedom to Fail: Heidegger's Anarchy*. Trans. Ian Alexander Moore and Christopher Turner. Malden, MA: Polity Press, 2015.

Waldenfels, Bernhard. *Topographie des Fremden: Studien zur Phänomenologie des Fremden* I. Frankfurt am Main: Suhrkamp Verlag, 1997.

Wolin, Richard. "National Socialism, World Jewry, and the History of Being: Heidegger's Black Notebooks." *Jewish Review of Books* (Summer 2014), http://jewishreviewofbooks.com/articles/993/national-socialism-world-jewry-and-the-history-of-being-heideggers-black-notebooks/.

Young-Bruehl, Elisabeth. *Hannah Arendt: For Love of the World*. New Haven, CT: Yale University Press, 2004.

Zaborowski, Holger. *"Eine Frage von Irre und Schuld?": Martin Heidegger und der Nationalsozialismus*. Frankfurt am Main: Fischer Verlag, 2010.

Zarader, Marlène. *The Unthought Debt: Heidegger and the Hebraic Heritage*. Trans. Bettina Bergo. Stanford: Stanford University Press, 2006.

Zimmerman, Hans Dieter. *Martin und Fritz Heidegger: Philosophie und Festnacht*. 2nd ed. Munich: C. H. Beck, 2005.

Zumbini, Massimo Ferrari. *Die Wurzeln des Bösen. Gründerjahre des Antisemitismus: Von der Bismarckzeit zu Hitler*. Frankfurt am Main: Klostermann Verlag, 2003.

NAME INDEX

////////////////////////////////

Adorno, Theodor W., 79
Alicke, Klaus-Dieter, 118n18
Aly, Götz, 121n41
Anaximander, 9–10
Arendt, Hannah, 1–2, 4, 28, 34, 65–
    68, 79–81, 85–87, 93, 97, 118n18,
    131n1, 131n4, 132n15
Aristotle, 12
Assmann, Jan, 134n27
Augustine, 76

Baumann, Gerhart, 110n2
Benz, Wolfgang, 110n6, 119n24
Biemel, Walter, 64
Blochmann, Elisabeth, 1, 65
Brock, Werner, 1, 65
Buber, Martin, 109n2, 116n8
Burkert, Walter, 113n19

Celan, Paul, 1, 66, 79, 87, 126n17,
    135n1
Cohen, Hermann, 15, 114n28
Cohn, Jonas, 65

Darwin, Charles, 29, 121n3
Democritus, 73
Derrida, Jacques, 1, 110n3
Di Cesare, Donatella, 109n1, 112n12
Dietze, Constantin von, 127n28
Diner, Dan, 121n47
Domarus, Max, 114n29, 119n31,
    119n32

Epicurus, 73
Eucken, Walter, 61, 127n25, 127n28
Euclid, 22

Farías, Victor, 125n17
Faye, Emmanuel, 112n12, 129n8
Fichte, Johann Gottlieb, 132n20
Frankl, Viktor E., 134n5
Freud, Sigmund, 26, 119n22
Friedländer, Paul, 80

Gagarin, Yuri, 74–75, 109n5
Geulen, Christian, 117n17, 121n1
Gobineau, Arthur de, 121n3